Battleground Europe

SAINT QUENTIN

1914-1918

Other guides in the Battleground Europe Series:

Walking the Salient *by* Paul Reed
Ypres - Sanctuary Wood and Hooge *by* Nigel Cave
Ypres - Hill 60 *by* Nigel Cave
Ypres - Messines Ridge *by* Peter Oldham
Ypres - Polygon Wood *by* Nigel Cave
Ypres - Passchendaele *by* Nigel Cave
Ypres - Airfields and Airmen *by* Michael O'Connor

Walking the Somme *by* Paul Reed
Somme - Gommecourt *by* Nigel Cave
Somme - Serre *by* Jack Horsfall & Nigel Cave
Somme - Beaumont Hamel *by* Nigel Cave
Somme - Thiepval *by* Michael Stedman
Somme - La Boisselle *by* Michael Stedman
Somme - Fricourt *by* Michael Stedman
Somme - Carnoy-Montauban *by* Graham Maddocks
Somme - Pozieres *by* Graham Keech
Somme - Courcelette *by* Paul Reed
Somme - Boom Ravine *by* Trevor Pidgeon
Somme - Mametz Wood *by* Michael Renshaw
Somme - Delville Wood *by* Nigel Cave
Somme - Advance to Victory (North) 1918 *by* Michael Stedman

Arras - Vimy Ridge *by* Nigel Cave
Arras - Gavrelle *by* Trevor Tasker and Kyle Tallett
Arras - Bullecourt *by* Graham Keech
Arras - Monchy le Preux *by* Colin Fox

Hindenburg Line *by* Peter Oldham
Hindenburg Line Epehy *by* Bill Mitchinson
Hindenburg Line Riqueval *by* Bill Mitchinson
Hindenburg Line Villers-Plouich *by* Bill Mitchinson
Hindenburg Line - Cambrai *by* Jack Horsfall & Nigel Cave
Hindenburg Line - Saint Quentin *by* Helen McPhail and Philip Guest

La Bassée - Neuve Chapelle *by* Geoffrey Bridger

Mons *by* Jack Horsfall and Nigel Cave

Accrington Pals Trail *by* William Turner

Poets at War: Wilfred Owen *by* Helen McPhail and Philip
Poets at War: Edmund Blunden *by* Helen McPhail and Phil

Gallipoli *by* Nigel Steel

Italy - Asiago *by* Francis Mackay

Boer War - The Relief of Ladysmith *by* Lewis Child
Boer War - The Siege of Ladysmith *by* Lewis Child
Boer War - Kimberley *by* Lewis Childs
Isandhlwana *by* Ian Knight and Ian Castle
Rorkes Drift *by* Ian Knight and Ian Castle

WW2 **Pegasus Bridge/Merville Battery** *by* Carl Shill
WW2 **Gold Beach** *by* Christopher Dunphie & Garry Joh
WW2 **Omaha Beach** *by* Tim Kilvert-Jones
WW2 **Battle of the Bulge - St Vith** *by* Michael Tolhu
WW2 **Dunkirk** *by* Patrick Wilson
WW2 **Calais** *by* John Cooksey
WW2 **March of *Das Reich* to Normandy** *by* Philip Vic
WW2 **Hill 112** *by* Tim Saunders

Battleground Europe Series guides under contract for future relea...

Somme - High Wood *by* Terry Carter
Somme - Ginchy *by* Michael Stedman
Somme - Combles *by* Paul Reed
Somme - Beaucourt *by* Michael Renshaw
Walking Arras *by* Paul Reed
Hougoumont *by* Julian Paget and Derek Saunders

Battleground Europe
SAINT QUENTIN
1914-1918

Helen McPhail & Philip Guest

Series editor
Nigel Cave

LEO COOPER

First published in 2000 by
LEO COOPER
an imprint of
Pen & Sword Books Limited
47 Church Street, Barnsley, South Yorkshire S70 2AS

ISBN 0 85052 789 9

A CIP catalogue of this book is available
from the British Library

Printed by Redwood Books Limited
Trowbridge, Wiltshire

CONTENTS

The road to St. Quentin.

INTRODUCTION

The German conquest of France in 1871 prompted a thorough review of the British Army. When Britain declared war on Germany on 4 August 1914, the British Expeditionary Force (B.E.F.) was mobilised rapidly and by 12 August Sir John French was able to take this small but highly trained force to France and onwards into Belgium to support Britain's allies against the invading German army.

When war broke out in the summer of 1914, Saint-Quentin was a proud and ancient city, home to around 65,000 people, a prosperous manufacturing and commercial centre. Dominated by the cathedral built between the twelfth and fifteenth centuries, with the tomb of the martyr St Quentin in its crypt, the city stands beside the River Somme and marks the junction of five main roads; and the Saint Quentin canal, built under the Emperor Napoleon between 1802 and 1810, links the rivers Seine and Escaut.

This setting has had a double influence on the city's history. The excellent access and the site north-west of Laon, within easy reach of the great industrial areas of the north and north-east, have always encouraged trade and communications - but all too frequently it has brought war to the Saint-Quentinois. The great siege of 1557 is noted on the vast war memorial close to the station, and the French and German armies clashed here during the Franco-Prussian war of 1870, shortly before the general armistice in 1871.

In the summer of 1914 the city's location once more set it at the centre of great historical drama, and memories of the earlier conflict surged back in response to the fresh invasion. The invading German troops were quick to spot possible snipers and made it all too clear that resistance to the invasion was useless. Civilians fled, crowding the roads with their handcarts, baggage, children, animals, best possessions. Any real or imagined attempt by snipers to interrupt the advance resulted in blazing houses, dead civilians and general destruction. Although many French families managed to flee ahead of the troops, together with thousands of Belgian refugees from the earliest days of the German invasion, many more were unable or unwilling to leave.

In the years after the Armistice, how many thousands of British families would have proud or bitter reason to remember the name of Saint Quentin? At least eight Divisions, 23 Brigades, 74 Battalions... an enormous number of fighting men, a weight of experience, courage, defeat and victory, all to be traced through these fields and villages

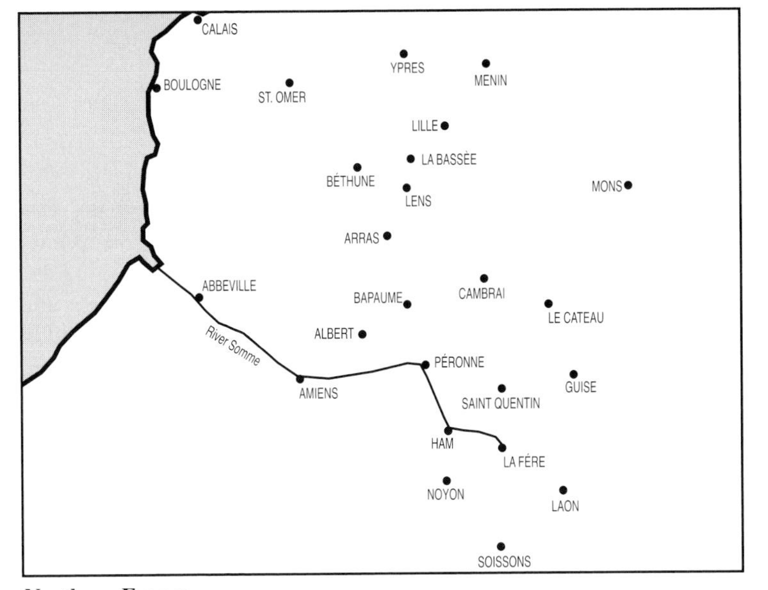

Northern France.

round the city. There is much to honour here.

In view of the considerable British presence around Saint Quentin, it may seem strange that the region has received little attention from the modern flood of visitors to the Western Front, for it is easy to reach and explore. This illustrated account of life in and around the city, the experience of both British troops and French forces and civilians, and the effect of the Hindenburg Line defences curving close round the outskirts, owes much to the modern French residents of Saint Quentin. We are particularly grateful to contributions, both historical documents and illustrations, from local individuals and organisations who are anxious to revisit their own history and to honour both their own forebears and the English military units who fought, died or survived so close to the city centre.

It is good to know that this extensive contribution and final triumph are remembered locally, as can be seen in the pages of a new French account of Saint Quentin during the Great War.[1] To gain a complete picture of what it felt like - whether British or French - to be in or near Saint Quentin in 1914-1918, we need to look at both sides of the Hindenburg Line and remember that the thousands of French civilians depended on the thousands of British troops to liberate them. As the war began in the turbulent movement and battles of 1914, surely no one in Saint Quentin could have foreseen the desperate fighting outside the city, or the four years of occupation that awaited them.

Helen McPhail, Philip Guest

1. *Sur les traces de la Grande Guerre dans la region de Saint-Quentin*, published in 2000. It includes contributions from English organisations and was financed by the city authorities. See Bibliography for details.

ACKNOWLEDGEMENTS

This account of the full spectrum of events around the city throughout the war could not have been written or illustrated without help from French sources: we were very fortunate in being able to draw on the knowledge, patience and energy of several individuals and organisations who went to great lengths to provide us with information and illustrations. Their contribution was an encouragement as we assembled material for this account of allied armies, and emphasised the value of looking beyond the traditional British focus. In particular we thank Madame Séverin, representing the Société Académique de Saint-Quentin, and Michel Dutoit, representing the Atelier mémoire Saint-Jean et La Croix.

Illustration credits:

Sous la Botte, histoire de la ville de Saint-Quentin pendant l'occupation allemande, Elie Fleury, Saint Quentin, 1925: pp

Société Académique de Saint-Quentin: pp. 23, 44, 53, 65, 85, 103, 108, 110, 111, 119,121, 127, 136, 137, 140, 143, 144,

Atelier mémoire Saint-Jean et La Croix: pp.16, 30, 32, 39, 41, 42, 49, 58, 75, 118, 139, 141, 142

Le Mémorial, Essigny-le-Grand: pp. 82, 131

R. Pike: p. 35

Saint Quentin before the war - ***the old port***

SERIES EDITOR'S INTRODUCTION

St Quentin is a sector of the British Front that is not as well visited as it deserves. Perhaps today's traveller is put off by the motorways that sweep around this impressive and ancient city. It is to be hoped that this book will encourage more to venture from the 'security' of the old 1916 Somme battlefield and to find a new area rich in heroism and endevour.

St Quentin is perhaps most remembered for a famous incident in the Retreat from Mons in 1914 when Major Tom Bridges, with an assistant, used a toy drum and a whistle to encourage men of two battalions – exhausted and disheartened – to pick themselves up and continue their seemingly endless retreat towards Paris.

Certainly, after the momentous events of that late summer, British troops were not to come near the city for many months. The German withdrawal to the Hindenburg line in the early months, of 1917 was to bring them back that way again. The brilliant initial sucess of the German Spring Offensive in March 1918 against Gough's Fifth Army brought the town once more into prominence. Best known of all the participants in that battle near here is probably Colonel Elstob VC, commemorated on the Pozières Memorial, and his famous stand with his men on Manchester Hill.

But there is far more to the fighting around here than isolated incidents and individuals. Philip Guest and Helen McPhail have brought numbers of people to this battlefield in tours that they have led; the combination of Philip's knowledge of the ground and the units involved and Helen' s research into the French records of the period provide a fascinating story.

St Quentin's place in the great war deserves to be better understood. The book also provides an opportunity – which has been seized – to extend our knowledge, in particular of the role of the French army and the local inhabitants in those events getting on for a century ago.

With the publication of this work much of the southern part of the Hindenburg line has now been covered in this series – St Quentin, Riqueval, Epehy and Villers-Plouich. It is encouraging to see also a future awareness amoungst the local French authorities of the importance of their history during such troubled years. It is to be hoped these books will help to encourage a trend in the historiography of the Great War to move on from the events of the 1916 Battle of the Somme to other periods of this the greatest conflict of British arms up to that time. The soldiers of 1914, 1917 and 1918 are as deserving of study as are the men of 1916.

Nigel Cave, Sacro Monte Calvario, Domodossola. September, 2000.

Chapter One

THE ROAD SOUTH

Crowded and uncomfortable, the troop trains carried the British units from the channel ports across northern France to Mons, the focus of its immediate concentration. The troops appreciated the enthusiastic welcome that met them along the route which included towns such as Saint Quentin and Le Cateau; but by the end of the same month these cheering French residents would see with alarm the same troops retreating desperately to the south.

Despite its brave efforts to hold the line at Mons, with 70,000 British troops facing 150,000 Germans, by the night of 23 August orders were issued for the B.E.F. to retire - the beginning of a famous retreat. Several Victoria Crosses were won here, including those awarded to Lieutenant Dease and Private Godley for their defence of the railway bridge at Nimy; Godley was the first private soldier of the Great War to receive a V.C.

It was the British II Corps, commanded by Lieutenant General Sir Horace Smith-Dorrien, which bore the brunt of the fighting, suffering some 4,000 casualties. Originally this command was to be in the hands of Lieutenant General Sir James Grierson, but on 17 August the General suddenly collapsed and died in the train taking him to the front. French's preference was for Sir Herbert Plumer to take Grierson's place, but Kitchener, the Secretary of State for War, sent Smith-Dorrien instead; the bad feeling between French and Smith-Dorrien was not helped by the decision to make a stand at Le Cateau, and it eventually resulted in Smith-Dorrien giving up his command early in May 1915, handing over to Plumer.

The Bridge at Mons where Lieutenant Dease and Private Godley of the 4th Royal Fusiliers won their Victoria Crosses on 23 August 1914.

The Casteau Road, Mons. The first and last shots fired by the B.E.F. in the Great War are marked by plaques on opposite sides of the Mons - Casteau road. The 1914 plaque, which is becoming blurred, reads: 'This tablet is erected to commemorate the action of C Squadron 4th Royal Irish Dragoon Guards on 22nd August 1914 when Corporal E. Thomas fired the first shot for the British Expeditionary Force and Captain C. B. Hornby led the first mounted attack against the Germans.' By 27 August the Squadron under Major Bridges' command was in Saint Quentin encouraging the stragglers of the Warwicks and Dublin Fusiliers to continue.

Sir John French

Smith-Dorrien's decision to make a stand at Le Cateau set up a controversy which was to continue until the death of the Commander in Chief, Sir John French, in 1925. (In 1926 Smith-Dorrien unveiled a memorial at Le Cateau, known as the Suffolk Memorial, in honour of the men of the Suffolks and other regiments who fell in the epic rearguard action there on 26 August 1914. By odd coincidence, one of the German regiments attacking the 2nd Battalion Suffolk Regiment that day carried the battle honour 'Gibraltar' on their badges - an honour also given to the Suffolks who had fought alongside the German regiment in the Gibraltar campaigns of 1779-83.)

After the stand at Le Cateau on 26 August, troops of Smith-Dorrien's II Corps, tired and battered, headed south towards Saint Quentin and beyond it. In the view of their commander his retreating Corps resembled 'a crowd leaving a race meeting', but by 28 August they had covered 35 miles, marching straight for the Somme. After their strenuous battle at Le Cateau it seems likely that if the Germans had pressed home their advantage and forced the British to fight again, II Corps would have faced possible defeat - fortunately, the German commanders did not fully appreciate the British plight and their pursuit was ineffective. Tired and somewhat disorganised, the British

LE CATEAU. The cenotaph commemorates the actions near its site on 26 August 1914, involving the Suffolk and Manchester regiments together with the Argyll & Sutherland Highlanders and various artillery units.

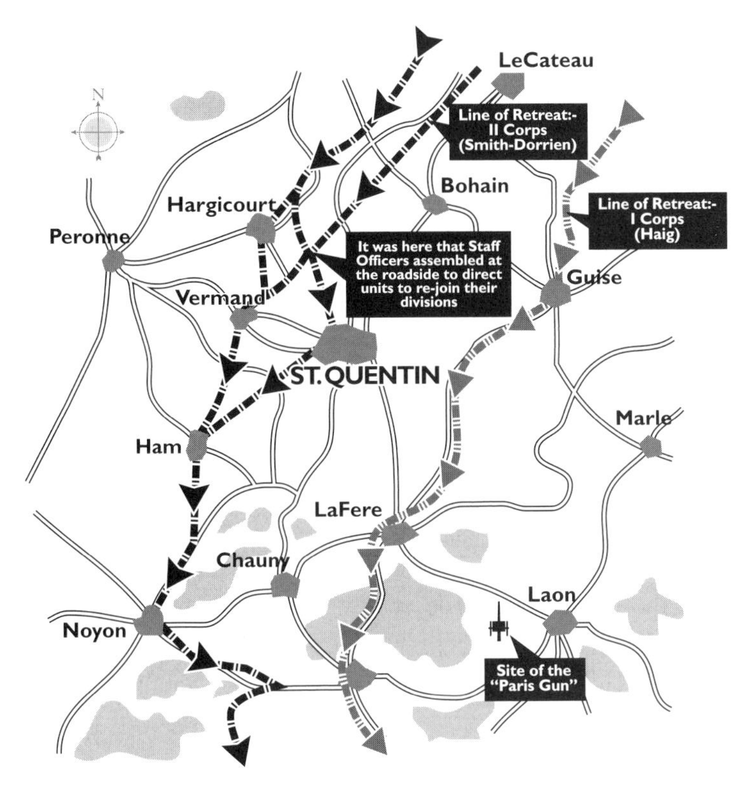

The retreat from Mons: from Le Cateau via Saint Quentin and Vermand, 26-27 August 1914 (Note the site of 'the Paris gun' which fired its first shot on Paris on 23 March 1918. The Kaiser stopped briefly in Saint Quentin on his way to the gun site, and spoke to captured British soldiers.)

troops plodded southwards. The timely arrival of some staff officers brought support and experience, saving what could easily have become a disorganised force as they directed the weary men and enabled them to rejoin their units. Another potential disaster was further avoided by the decision of Sir William Robertson, Quartermaster General, to have military stores and rations dumped along the route of the withdrawal.

During the morning of 26 August both General Headquarters and Corps Headquarters were directing operations from Saint Quentin, with Sir John French, the Commander in Chief, operating from part of the elegant Henri Martin school off the Boulevard Richelieu. As two divisions streamed down the road from Saint Quentin it was clear that their arrival on the edge of the city would cause even greater congestion; so staff officers took post along the approach roads and, as the retreating columns reached them, turned some away to the south-east into Saint Quentin while the rest made their way south-west towards Vermand.Inside Saint Quentin, General Sir John French held a conference in the morning of 26 August at his headquarters in the school, with three French generals - Joffre, d'Amade and Lanrezac, the latter at Joffre's request.

As a conference between allies, it was not a success, despite the urgency of the deteriorating situation. Sir John French was determined to continue the retreat, and relations between French and Lanrezac were not helped by the inability of either general to speak the other's language at all competently.

When French and his personal staff departed for Noyon, 25 miles to the south-west, he left his staff officers disheartened and full of gloom. The strain and confusion was becoming intolerable for the officers, and indeed the Chief of Staff suffered a temporary collapse. As Sir John French left he was apparently unable to offer any encouragement, and morale was badly affected.

French forces in the area, the 10th Territorial Infantry Regiment, awaited orders. Poorly equipped, they set out to intercept German patrols to the north of Saint Quentin - and found themselves facing powerfully armed advance parties from prestigious German units. From 26 August the 1st and 3rd Battalions were deployed to the north and east of Saint Quentin, seeing no German troops but plenty of British units as they withdrew. On 28 August their 2nd Battalion came under fire from more numerous and better equipped German troops between Levergies and Bellenglise: losses for the whole regiment that

The Henri Martin School, Saint Quentin. For a few days in August 1914 this was General French's headquarters: on 26 August French was in conference here with Generals Joffre, Lanrezac and d'Amade.

day came to 22 officers and over 1,900 men. They are commemorated by a monument in Bellenglise cemetery.

The British army continued to retreat down the roads from Le Cateau to Saint Quentin, crowded with weary soldiers in what one officer described as 'a blurred nightmare'. Others remembered falling asleep as they rode or walked, wrestling with the desire to fall out of the columns and give in to the desperate need for sleep. A lucky few managed to do so: the 2nd Royal Welch Fusiliers found a field where they could shelter against the corn stooks for a brief rest - but when the order came to move off quickly, some fifty men failed to hear it and were left behind.

Meanwhile, one of the units directed towards Vermand was the 1st Battalion East Lancashire Regiment, consisting of around 400 men, who crossed the Saint Quentin canal at Bellenglise and successfully avoided some 1,000 German cavalry to the west. At Vermand they found a little dry bread before continuing their travels, reaching the town of Ham late the next day, 27 August. In 26 hours the battalion had covered 35 miles without rations except what food they could find in the villages along the way: yet morale remained high as the men marched on, well nigh exhausted but still able to whistle and sing.

Another fortunate unit was the 1st East Surreys. Making their way south-west towards Riqueval, they discovered Geneve Farm (still there today) just off the main road, with spacious stables and outhouses, and as much straw as they wanted. The farmer refused all payment, requesting only that the senior officer should write to him occasionally. By 3 a.m. on 27 August the battalion was up and on the march again, reaching Saint Quentin just after mid-day.

The 2nd Battalion Suffolk Regiment had a harsher passage. The battalion stood fast at Le Cateau for nine hours, against a ceaseless storm of enemy fire, and was eventually overwhelmed by superior numbers. As the Suffolks arrived in Saint Quentin at dawn on 27 August the officer in command - a mere lieutenant - took the roll-call: only 111 men replied, some of them belonging to other regiments.

When the 1st Battalion Lincolnshire Regiment reached Vermand in the evening of 27 August they turned into the buildings of a large farm with plenty of water for washing and filling water-bottles, and the men were able to snatch a few hours' sleep: but they had no food. Throughout their retreat the Lincolnshires were told that rations would be issued 'at the next village' but, as their Quartermaster wrote in the regimental history, '"Next", like tomorrow, never comes'.

The 3rd Battalion Worcestershire Regiment were more fortunate:

THE GERMAN INVASION, 28-29 August 1914

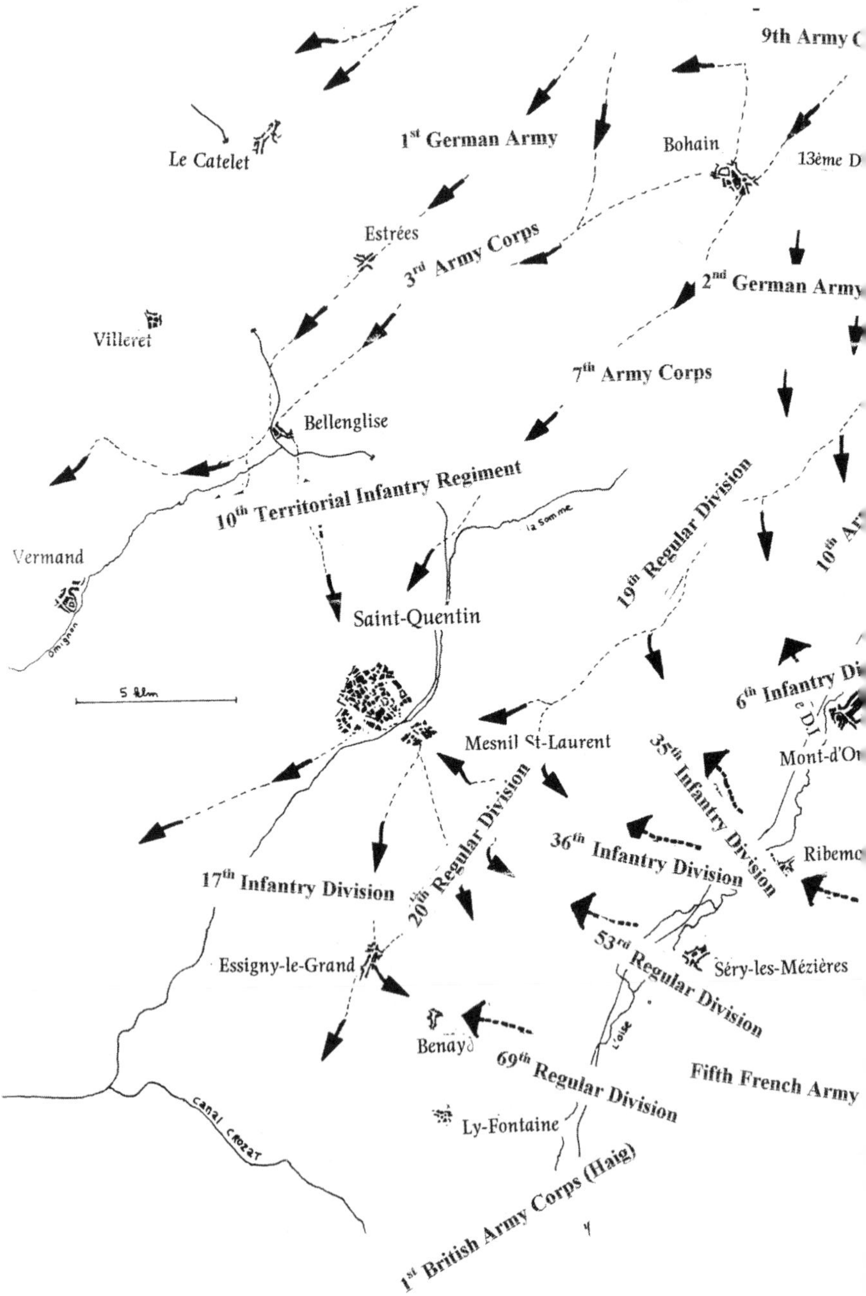

28 August: the French 10th Territorial Infantry Regiment confronts the German outposts at Bellenglise. 29 August: The Fifth French Army attacks towards Saint Quentin.

they reached Vermand ahead of the Lincolns, arriving during the afternoon of 27 August and were issued with supplies. There was transport for the sick and unfit, they were able to prepare for a night march, and by 4 a.m. the next morning they reached Ham, the Battalion's first sight of the River Somme.

Close behind them, the 2nd Battalion Royal Scots reached Vermand soon after, eager to push on through the town after their recent breakfast of bully beef, marmalade and biscuits. Because of the congestion on the roads they had stopped for a roadside sleep. They found Vermand still full of transport and guns, with the infantry waiting, patient or irritated, for the streets to clear. The Royal Scots eventually marched off, plodding through the night 'with limbs like lead' and sometimes 'through want of sleep the men in front seemed to be floating visions rather than beings of flesh and blood'.

They too reached Ham, continuing through it and lucky to 'capture' a supply of tea and fresh meat sufficient to feed the whole Battalion; there was no time to cook the meat before they were ordered onwards, so they took it with them - no other battalion fed so well that day.

Among the battalions directed to Saint Quentin were the 2nd Royal Welch Fusiliers, of the 19th Brigade, which witnessed the depressing sight of military equipment and some British army lorries abandoned by the roadside for lack of petrol.

The older form of army transport, the horses, were supplied with forage by the Army Service Corps Horse Transport units designated as 'trains', used to deliver ration supplies to the troops and carry their baggage as well as fodder for the horses. The 'train' allocated to the 19th Brigade under the command of a captain was a below-strength company made up of officers, NCOs and men, horses and vehicles of various types, hurriedly brought together from various A.S.C. (Army Service Corps) units wherever they could be found. Officers and men therefore barely knew each other and had had very little time to train together, but settled into an efficient unit and reached Mons on 23 August 1914. After the battle there they took part in the retreat to Le Cateau; here they were held up for several hours at the cross-roads leading to Saint Quentin whilst a continuous line of magnificently mounted French cavalry rode across the road, impressive with their shining metal breastplates and the plumes of horsehair streaming from their helmets. These were General Sordet's cavalry which had first seen action on 5 August in Belgium.

Once the road was clear again, the A.S.C. 'train' left Le Cateau for Saint Quentin. Before entering the town, on 26 August, it stopped whilst the captain in command went on by car to find the officer in charge of the main A.S.C. supply column. As he returned he met his 'train' galloping down the Saint Quentin road towards him, with men sitting beside the drivers who trained their rifles threateningly in all directions. It took the captain about a mile before he could stop the horses, and learned that a false order had been given to gallop off at full speed - a ruse by German sympathisers who were trying to scatter the transport column. The horses were calmed and given nose-bags and the captain left for the Henri Martin school to report to General Headquarters there: but GHQ had moved on by now, and was on its way to Noyon some 25 miles away.

When the A.S.C. 'train' entered the square by the Henri Martin school to await further orders they found a tall and magnificently uniformed French officer, part of a prestigious French cavalry unit; he was expecting the Germans to enter the town at any moment and was using the telephone frantically in his attempts to stop trainloads of French soldiers being sent in the direction of the Le Cateau area.

There was further confusion in the Square late that night (26 August), with General Smith-Dorrien trying to locate General French. He urgently needed to consult with his commander, but to his astonishment he learned that GHQ had left for Noyon. Following the A.S.C. captain, Smith-Dorrien was taken by car to the railway station where, fortunately, the telephone was working and Smith-Dorrien was able to re-establish contact with G.H.Q. Meanwhile the 'train' resumed its retreat, with Noyon their next stop.

Some of the retreating troops crossed the Saint Quentin canal near Riqueval, but the Royal Welch followed their instructions to turn left at this junction and to make their way into Saint Quentin itself. (It would be another four years before British troops returned to Riqueval.)

They lost very few men along the way and reached the city 'at breakfast time', soaked to the skin from the overnight rain, tired and hungry. The regimental transport had been lost, but the Battalion was halted opposite a grocer's shop and Lieutenant-Colonel Delmé Radcliffe, their commanding officer, requisitioned the shop's entire contents. The grocer was less than delighted, but accepted the requisition papers and handed over his stocks for distribution, and after a brief rest the battalion resumed its march.

On the northern edge of the city centre the park known as the Champs Elysées provided a useful open space where army supplies could be handed out, or approaching units receive directions. The army staff had placed large notice-boards at several junctions on the way into the city centre, and a blackboard at the junction of the rue Emile Zola and the entrance to the Place de l'Hôtel de Ville indicated the route for the retreating units to follow out of the city, on to the road to Ham and Noyon. The 2nd Royal Welch turned out of the square and continued their march southwards beside the canal, through Tugny and then for a brief stop at Ollezy.

Although the 2nd Royal Welch survived the retreat from Mons relatively unscathed, they undoubtedly shared the hardships of the long march, a journey which demanded a high degree of stamina. The weary tramp southwards throughout the stifling August heat was interrupted by periods of rain and cold - and the uncertainties and alarms of retreat were intensified by not knowing what was happening, seldom seeing enemy soldiers or understanding the reasons for the many changes of plan. All that the British troops could see were the numerous signs of disaster around them, and all they could do was continue their retreat.

The good fortune of the 2nd Royal Welch in avoiding battle casualties was not shared by the 1st Dorsetshire Regiment, the last battalion of the 5th Division to leave the battlefield at Mons, who suffered losses in rear-guard action as the retreat began. At Le Cateau they came under fire again before joining in the general withdrawal, and eventually entered Saint Quentin on 27 August.

They found the city carrying on its normal life, the streets crowded and the cafés open for business as usual. The Dorsets marched on through the city and halted briefly in a field close to the station before resuming their retreat, with two of the regimental drummers playing the flute. The battalion reached Ollezy later the same day, just south of the Somme, and bivouacked for the night; since the afternoon of the previous day they had marched some forty miles on congested roads with little to eat, in very hot weather - but the Dorsets were a well-disciplined battalion and were rightly proud of the achievement, with no stragglers and very few men falling out.

The Dorsets had no cover that night and no doubt envied the 1st Queen's Own Royal West Kent Regiment, which also bivouacked at Ollezy on 27 August. They too had reached Saint Quentin the same day, but arrived earlier and avoided the congested streets by marching straight through and halting briefly on the outskirts before continuing to billets 'for something more like a rest' at Ollezy.

Like the Royal Welch Fusiliers, the 1st Duke of Cornwall's Light Infantry had been re-directed at Bellenglise on to the Saint Quentin road. It was 5.30 a.m. on 27 August when they reached the city, exhausted and hungry after marching some seventeen miles the previous day as well as fighting. Unlike some units, the D.C.L.I. had retained its formation and earned personal congratulations from Sir John French as he stood at the roadside on the retreat, watching his battered army pass by. The Commander in Chief commended the battalion commander on the D.C.L.I.'s appearance, perfectly dressed in fours and keeping immaculate march displine, and remarked that at last a formed battalion had arrived. Later in the day they too marched on to Ollezy, by now part of the Brigade rearguard together with a battalion of the East Surrey Regiment.

In the final phase of the Battle of Mons, on 24 August, the extreme left of the British Army was held by the 1st Cheshire Regiment. Their companions in the fighting at Elouges/Audregnies were the 9th Lancers, the 4th Dragoon Guards, the 1st Norfolks, and 119th Battery Royal Field Artillery; two Victoria Crosses were won here, by Major E. W. Alexander of 119th Battery and Captain F. O. Grenfell of the 9th Lancers.

The 1st Cheshires suffered severe losses at Audregnies: of its 25 officers and 952 other ranks before the attack, only seven officers and 200 NCOs and men were present afterwards, and it was this very depleted Battalion which entered Saint Quentin on 26 August on its way to Ollezy. Yet the Battalion had achieved one triumph which could not come to its full conclusion for another four years: when it became clear that a miniature Regimental Colour, of which they were very proud, was inevitably going to be captured, one of the battalion drummers hid it in straw in the roof of a house. Another soldier, lying wounded in a convent, knew of the hiding place and persuaded the village priest and schoolmaster to recover it and look after it. As the war continued there were fears that it would be discovered by the occupying Germans, so it was taken to a local school, furled and placed in a metal pipe behind a bricked-up attic. By chance the battalion was very close to Audregnies at the Armistice in 1918, and a party of Cheshires was able to retrieve it.

In Saint Quentin itself, the local population was becoming increasingly worried by the sequence of events. They could see that the British troops would not remain long, and realised that the German forces were not far behind. From time to time the Place de l'Hôtel de Ville filled up with weary British soldiers, who formed up again after a brief rest and continued their trek southwards. The rifle shot fired into the air as one of these formations hastily prepared to leave understandably added to the air of unease and menace that was already affecting the people of Saint Quentin.

Chapter Two

THE COLONELS AND THE ALLIES - DEFEAT

All the regimental histories that describe battalions engaged in the fighting at Mons and the subsequent retreat stress the fact that officers and men were completely unable to rest and sleep, and in many cases to find food as they retreated. And as they marched away, supporting their wounded, their morale was put to a further test as they trudged to and fro, frequently without any idea of what was happening.

Many of the soldiers were Reservists, recalled to their regiments at the outbreak of war barely a month earlier and out of condition for long marches. The army issue boots were often ill-fitting and produced intensely painful blisters. Overcome with weariness, men frequently slept in their ranks as they marched along the pavé roads. And yet, somehow, officers and men alike kept going. The officers - tired, weary, hungry, some of them past the prime of life - had to take important decisions in difficult circumstances. Remarkably, men of all ranks seemed to find the endurance to overcome such challenges, although understandably there were exceptions, and some of these could be seen on 27 August in Saint Quentin in the Place Gaspard de Coligny, close to the Place de l'Hôtel de Ville.

The 1st Royal Warwickshire Regiment and the 2nd Royal Dublin Fusiliers were two splendid battalions forming part of 10th Infantry Brigade of the 4th Division. The Royal Warwicks were commanded by Lieutenant-Colonel J. F. Elkington, with the Dublin Fusiliers under the command of Lieutenant-Colonel A. E. Mainwaring, Elkington being the senior of the two. Both battalions had been involved in particularly severe fighting on 26 August during the BEF's retreat from Mons, in action to the west of Le Cateau around Ligny and Haucourt.

One of the 1st Royal Warwickshire's young officers in the battle was to make a great name for himself in later days: this was Lieutenant Bernard Law Montgomery, better known in the Second World War as Field-Marshal Viscount Montgomery of Alamein - 'Monty' - who was already showing signs of his natural independence of approach. In response to an enquiry from Montgomery as they left for active service, Elkington stated that money was not required in war because everything would be provided by the army; as the remnants of his Battalion left the battlefield at Le Cateau on 26 August, hungry and without supplies in their retreat towards Saint Quentin, Elkington perhaps regretted his prophecy; wisely, Montgomery had ignored his CO's advice.

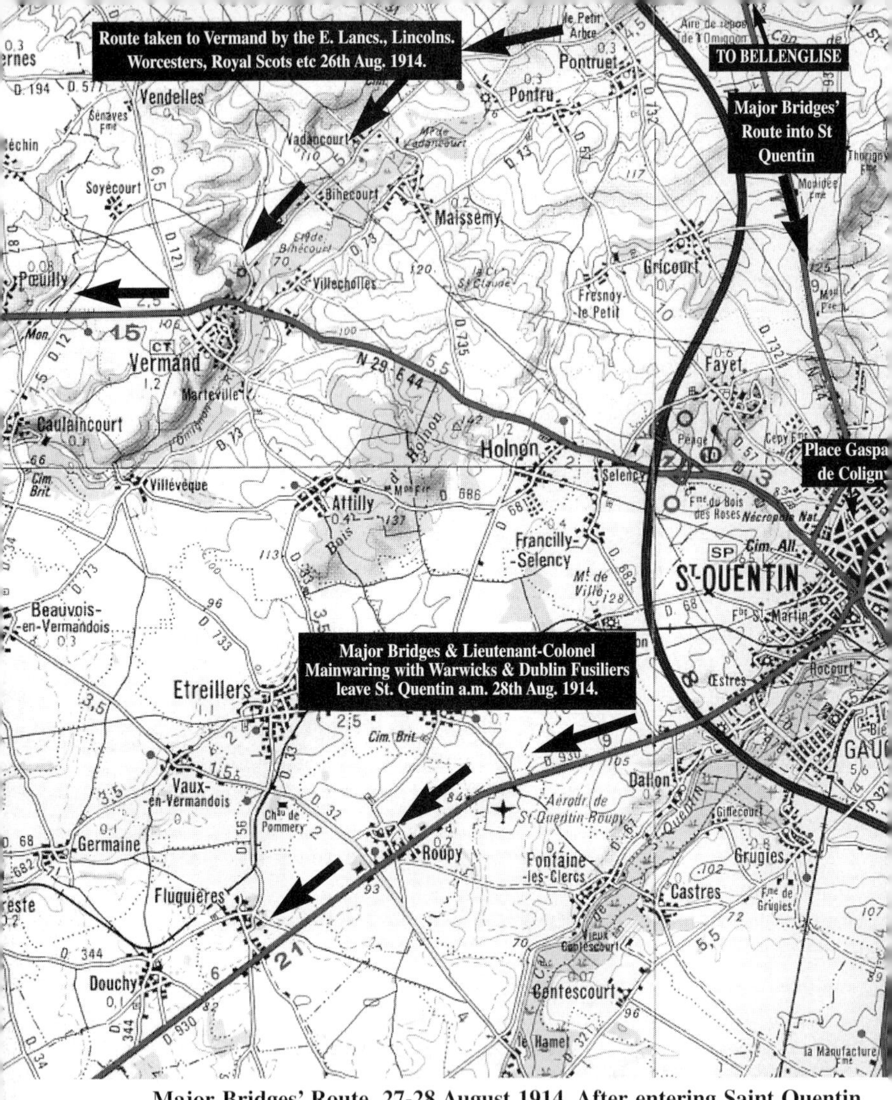

Major Bridges' Route, 27-28 August 1914. After entering Saint Quentin, Major Bridges left with the Warwickshires and the Dublin Fusiliers

The Warwickshires' battalion, some 600 strong, was between the retreating British and in front of the advancing Germans. All kit was burned to make room on the transport for the wounded and they set off in two parties, tired, hungry and in very low spirits. About half of the battalion reached Saint Quentin on 27 August under Lieutenant-Colonel Elkington, while Montgomery and the other half, under Major A. J. Poole, caught up with their Division on 28 August and set off by lorry transport to Compiègne. Montgomery never forgot the march from Le Cateau: he called it `the retreat from Moscow'.

Also en route for Saint Quentin was Major G. T. M. Bridges of the 4th (Royal Irish) Dragoon Guards, whose C Squadron under his command claimed to have fired the first British shot of the war on the continent, on 22 August 1914 at Mons.

As he and his men rode into the Place Gaspard de Coligny in Saint Quentin on the afternoon of 27 August, they found the whole square full of British soldiers wandering about, aimless and exhausted or fast asleep, lying full length on the pavement. They were men of Elkington's 1st Royal Warwicks and Mainwaring's 2nd Royal Dublin Fusiliers, who had been among the last to arrive in the city. Bridges was astounded at the sight, and sought an explanation: he discovered that Elkington and Mainwaring had given a written undertaking to Dr Muller, the Mayor of Saint Quentin, that they would not endanger the inhabitants' safety by fighting in the city. The two officers, battle weary and thoroughly exhausted, Mainwaring certainly sick, obviously unable to think coherently and convinced that their men had reached the limit of their endurance, had decided that it would be proper to sign the undertaking.

Bridges, however, recovered the document, and set about getting the men of both Battalions on their feet and on the march again.

It seemed an impossible task, but Bridges, driven perhaps by desperation, found inspiration: with some toy musical instruments acquired from a local shop he formed an impromptu military band. Marching round and round the large and impressive well-head in the square, the 'musicians' and their penny whistles and drum roused the weary men until, formed into a line of troops with the Major at its head, they set off out of the city to safety. The Mayor provided a guide to lead the way and, armed with a walking-stick, Lieutenant-Colonel Mainwaring marched wearily alongside Major

A famous well head. Major Bridges assembled tired and exhausted men of the Warwicks and Dublin Fusiliers by marching round the well-head with improvised music, before marching out of the city. The well-head was moved from the Place Gaspard de Coligny in 1965 and re-established close to the Place Hotel de Ville

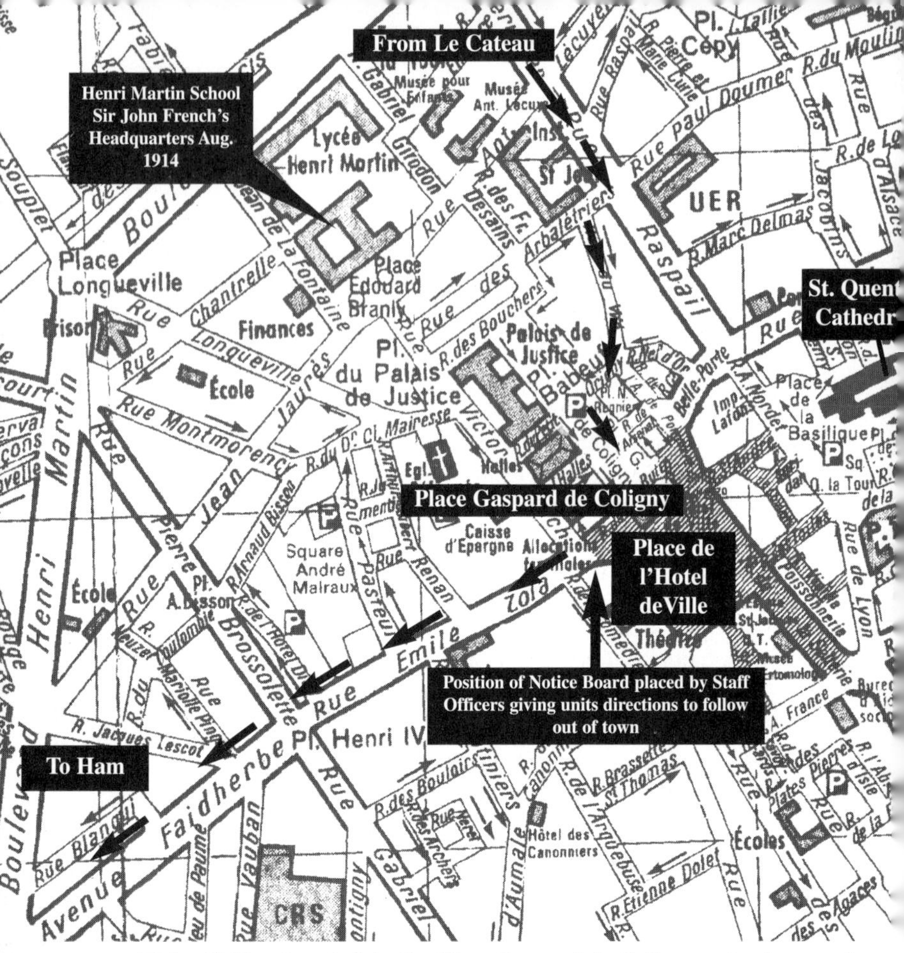

Major Bridges' route into the Place Gaspard de Coligny and subsequent departure with the Warwicks and Dublin Fusiliers, 27-28 August, 1914.

Bridges. By 2 a.m. on 28 August the line of men reached Roupy. Lieutenant-Colonel Elkington, on the other hand, had apparently disappeared.

By 28 August 1914, German troops had entered the town and, as in 1871, it was totally in the invaders' hands. Perhaps fortunately, no one could know how long the occupation would last, and it seemed that for some at least the fighting French spirit of the population of Saint Quentin was undimmed. As one diarist wrote of a friend, 'Il ne doute pas de la victoire', although such confidence was to be severely tested in the long trial to be endured until November 1918.

A patrol of Uhlans reached the railway station on the south-eastern outskirts of the city, and demanded surrender. Later, the German cavalry left the railway station and made their way up the rue de l'Isle to

German soldiers in the place Hôtel de Ville during the occupation.

the rue des Jacobins near the cathedral. With pointed helmets shining, bulky greatcoats covering their uniforms and carrying lances across their backs, they presented an alarming picture; one French observer who saw the cavalry trotting past described them as Attila's horsemen - barbarians from afar, their horses' hooves pounding the city's pavé streets. By nightfall the whole of Saint Quentin was completely silent.

The German army headquarters was in no doubt about their success: 'The defeat of the English is complete'. They went on to attribute 'the latest defeat of the English near Saint Quentin' to the actions of their 'masses of cavalry pursuing the English towards Saint Quentin' and asserted that the British were 'now completely cut off from their communications and can no longer escape by the ports at which they disembarked'. During the next four years they made every effort to confirm this statement, and sometimes it seemed that they would achieve it. There were many reasons why they did not succeed in the

The Occupation. Watched by a crowd of mainly German military personnel, a guard-changing ceremony appears to be taking place in front of the Hôtel de Ville; with a similar modern view of the building.

end, but one of them must have been the endurance and fighting capabilities of the British soldier which the Germans had so recently experienced along the roads to Saint Quentin: the city and the German army were to see those same qualities over and over again in this area in the years to come.

In due course Major Bridges handed the surrender notes, signed by the two colonels, to a superior officer, and on 12 September 1914 both Elkington and Mainwaring appeared before courts martial. At the end of their trials both were sentenced to be cashiered because they had agreed to surrender themselves and their troops without due cause.

Mainwaring and Elkington were both sons of army officers who had eventually reached the rank of general. Although with hindsight it is easy to criticise their actions, it seems likely that the regimental tradition that the welfare of their men and the prevention of unnecessary loss of life should always be a priority, combined with physical exhaustion and lack of sleep (Mainwaring had had no sleep for more than three days), affected their judgement.

After his court martial, Mainwaring returned to England a sick man. Little is known of how he spent the years following his dismissal from the army, although he prepared a statement of explanation of his conduct at Saint Quentin and had friends who tried to help him. His health failed seriously in the late 1920s and he died in 1930 at the age of 66.

Lieutenant-Colonel Elkington's eventual reinstatement and military rehabilitation are remarkable in contrast. He too returned to England after his court martial but then moved to Paris and joined the French Foreign Legion, serving with them in their actions at Vimy Ridge and Souchez in 1915. Later that year he took part in the Legion's attack on Navarin Farm, near Rheims, and was severely wounded in the leg. After many months in a French hospital he was discharged from the Legion, having been awarded the Médaille Militaire and the Croix de Guerre.

Sir Aylmer Hunter-Weston, who had presided at Elkington's court martial, took steps for his reinstatement in his regiment and later the King approved his appointment to the Distinguished Service Order. His wounds precluded further military service; he retired from the army in 1919 and died in 1944.

The French armies were on the move too. On 27 August, the day after the conference at the Henri Martin school in Saint Quentin, General Joffre sent for General Lanrezac of the French Fifth Army to meet him in Laon, 32 miles to the south-east. Despite Lanrezac's objections, Joffre ordered him to mount an attack on the enemy on a line Guise to Saint Quentin. The Battle of Guise began early on 29 August and was successful, although progress towards Saint Quentin quickly proved to be impossible.

Yet all was not in vain: for, with his forces elsewhere compelled to retreat, the German General Von Bülow recorded that his men 'were exhausted by the Battle of Guise and unable to pursue'.

French forces in the area, the 10th Territorial Infantry Regiment, awaited orders. Poorly equipped, they set out to intercept German patrols to the north of Saint Quentin - and found themselves facing powerfully armed advance parties from prestigious German units. General Lanrezac, commanding the French Fifth army, was now required to attack towards Saint Quentin from the east, while at the same time looking out for the possible arrival of German troops from Guise. Part of the army crossed the River Oise, at Ribemont, Séry-les Mézières and Marcy, while the rest remained near Guise. After violent confrontations the former groups withdrew so that the Fifth Army would not be isolated by the growing numbers of German troops. Despite this withdrawal, the operation was considered a success since it forced the German forces to turn away from their set route to pursue the French Fifth army.

Battles of Saint Quentin and Guise, 29 August 1914.

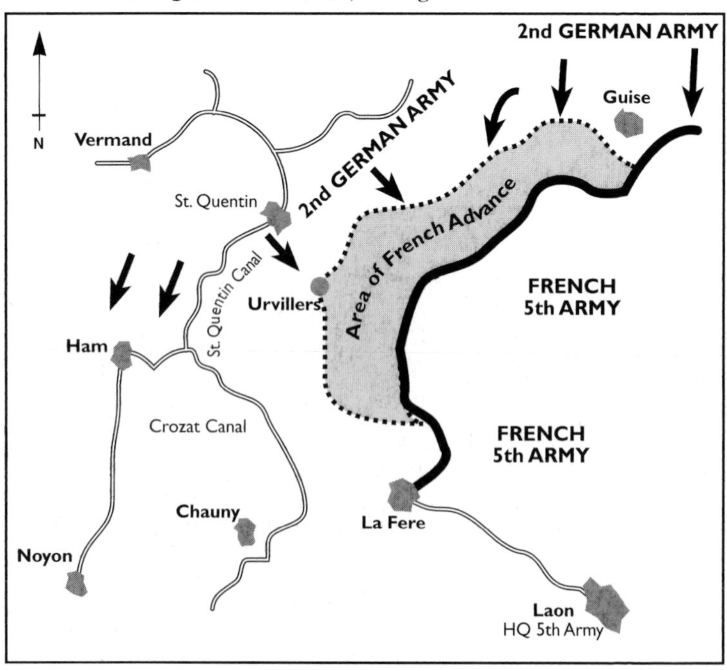

While General Smith-Dorrien's II Corps retreated from Mons and made its way to Saint Quentin and beyond, General Sir Douglas Haig's command, I Corps, was similarly in retreat but following a different route. Originally Haig had been ordered to cross over to Saint Quentin, but in the event I Corps moved south towards Landrecies and Guise, eventually passing some nine miles to the east of Saint Quentin to reach the Forest of Saint Gobain on 29 August 1914.

On 25 August the Corps reached Landrecies, where the 3rd Coldstream Guards was involved in a rearguard action. It seems that Haig never forgot Landrecies - among other, perhaps more serious, events, he apparently left his watch with a local watchmaker for repairs, returning in 1918 to claim it (without success).

Apart from this rearguard action in Landrecies, I Corps experienced very little activity during the retreat, in strong contrast to their

The Allies in Retreat 25 - 31 August 1914. The French armies' efforts to delay the German advance were successful at Guise but they were unable to reach Saint Quentin, which the British had left early on the morning of 27 August. By 31 August the British line of retreat had reached the River Aisne

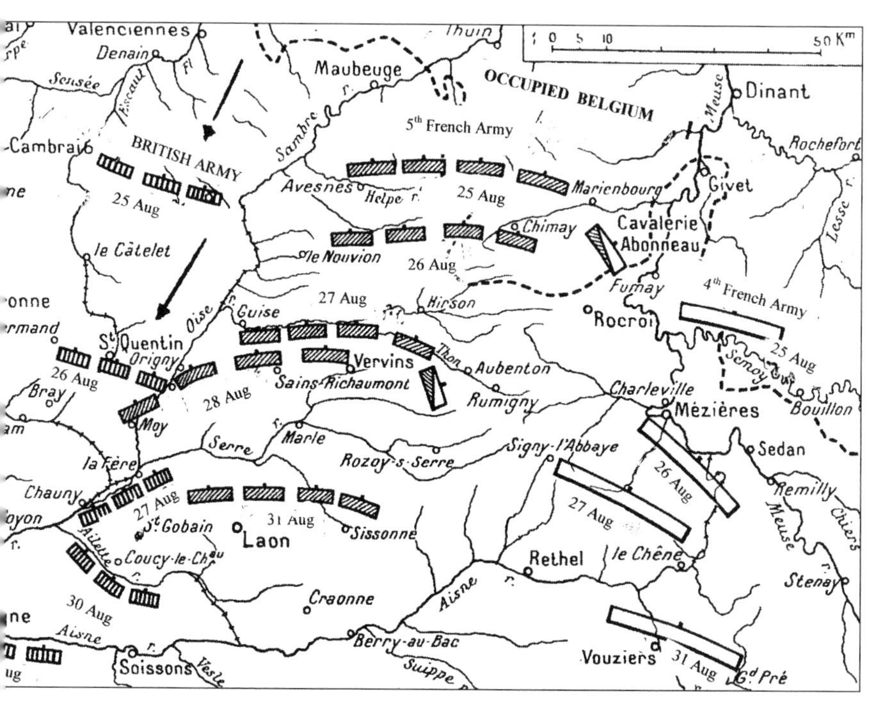

comrades in II Corps who were streaming wearily down the roads leading south out of Saint Quentin. Indeed, some of Haig's troops had yet to fire a shot. During their continued march southwards, I Corps was told that they were taking part in a 'strategic withdrawal', an explanation that they found difficult to accept. They had expected to fight and were bewildered, but by 7 September their expectations were rewarded as the retreat came to an end. The Battle of the Marne was followed by the Allies' advance to the Aisne; both sides 'dug in' - and the trench warfare that was to become so familiar was about to begin.

The German Memorial at Senercy. This simple stone commemorates the German and French soldiers who died in the battles for Guise and Saint Quentin, August 1914.

Chapter Three

OCCUPATION

On 29 August posters appeared, bearing the signature of the German Commandant, stating that henceforth the city was under the German military and ordering the surrender of all arms and equipment. Meanwhile, interminable columns of German soldiers stepped out cheerfully along the long road leading northwards out of the city, singing to the rhythm of their marching and clearly intoxicated with the scale of their recent victory.

It did not take long for the German army to take over buildings which had so recently served the needs of the British army. Following General French's departure for new headquarters in Noyon, the Henri Martin School had been used as a British casualty clearing station and until mid-morning on 27 August, when the last train left, the most severely wounded British soldiers were sent on from there by ambulance train, using Saint Quentin railway station. When the school was

The canal at Saint Quentin. A sketch in war-time, before the trees along the canal banks were felled, either for fuel or for military purposes.

The Palais de Fervaques. During the retreat in August 1914, food and drink was handed out to the passing British soldiers from the broad steps and the building was used as a temporary hospital.

taken over by the German army as they occupied the city, the medical supplies and equipment abandoned by the British were immediately put to use.

Another building that was promptly commandeered by the invading Germans was the Palais de Fervaques in the rue Victor Basch. It was from the broad flight of steps of this building that British army food supplies were distributed to the British troops as they passed through Saint Quentin on their way to Ham. The Germans later used it to accommodate wounded British and French prisoners, but as they failed to provide medical facilities it fell to the Sisters of Charity to provide nursing care for the sick and wounded men.

Irksome regulations were published, some very ominous - for instance, all men aged between 18 and 48 had to register with the German authorities. A curfew operated from 7 p.m. and nobody was allowed to leave the city. In November, German troops began a search of all cellars, confiscating any wine that they found on the pretext that it was needed for their ambulances. The cold weather created a shortage of coal, and coal merchants were instructed by the Mayor to conserve their stocks. A levy of 220,000 francs was imposed on the town, with threats of dire consequences if the money was not quickly forthcoming.

The Place du 8 Octobre, during the occupation and today. The first German troops to enter Saint Quentin in 1914 came over the bridge beyond the houses behind the statue.

The whole character of Saint Quentin was changed as it became a local German capital, the headquarters of the German Second Army with a general in command assisted by a Town Major.

Major Bridges and his column may have left Saint Quentin with the remnants of the Royal Warwicks and Dublin Fusiliers, but there were still some stragglers left in the city who did not get away with him. These included No. 10825 Private Thomas Hands of the 1st King's Own and No. 10234 Private John Hughes of the 2nd Royal Irish Rifles.

The 1st King's Own had suffered severely at Le Cateau on 26

Two views of the monument to the siege of 1557 stripped of its bronzes, and showing the damaged cathedral, a view opened out by destruction around it. A military photograph, and an artist's version showing local people returning after the Armistice (painted by Jean Lefort in December 1918).

August 1914. The battalion had been holding a line in front of Haucourt and forward of Elkington's 1st Royal Warwicks and Mainwaring's 2nd Dublin Fusiliers. Mistakenly they had believed that the French were covering the positions in front of them and had decided to delay digging trenches and go to sleep instead, a decision which was to cost them dear.

At 6 a.m. they came under overwhelming enemy machine-gun fire as some 5,000 men of a German cavalry divison and two battalions of German infantry fell upon them. The result was predictable. Despite the ready assistance of the Royal Warwicks, the King's Own took heavy casualties, including the death of their commanding officer, Lieutenant-Colonel Dykes. Private Hands must somehow have lost touch with his battalion during the retreat from Le Cateau (when it was directed north of Saint Quentin) and found himself alone in Saint Quentin instead.

Both soldiers were hidden by the French and given civilian clothes, a kind gift with deadly consequences. Private Hands regularly went out alone in the town, quarrelling with German soldiers and eventually striking up a friendship with a local girl, despite warnings from those who had taken him in. The warnings were justified, for eventually this pretty girl reported the existence of the two British fugitives to the authorities for the sake of the reward they offered.

Not only were the two soldiers arrested, but the French families with whom they had been living were arrested too and suffered harsh retribution; Gustave Preux, a weaver and one of the generous householders who provided shelter, was deported to hard labour in Germany and returned after the war in broken health. At their trial, the protection of the Hague Convention was put forward as a defence by the two men, but as they were discovered in civilian clothes the Germans deemed them to be British spies, and both were sentenced to death.

Hughes and Hands were executed on 8 March 1915. In the hours between verdict and execution, the two men roamed the prison where they were held, singing Irish songs. Private Hughes, the

Grave of Thomas Hands. He is buried next to John Hughes, executed with him, in Saint Quentin Northern Communal Cemetery.

1870 Memorial in the Communal Cemetery showing the damage caused by shelling in 1914-18.

Irishman, wanted to wear a shamrock as he faced the firing squad, but had to make do with a bunch of violets delivered by his hostess, Madame Preux, which he pinned to his cap. After the execution the bodies of Hughes and Hands were buried in Saint Quentin Northern Communal cemetery and buried together (plot 19, row E, graves 10 and 11). The girl who denounced them was arrested and tried after the war, and sentenced to death in 1921.

The autumn and winter months of 1914-15 saw several other discoveries of British soldiers in the area, followed by execution. At Guise, to the east of Saint Quentin, eleven British soldiers were shot. Left behind there as Haig's I Corps retreated through the town, they were taken in and cared for; their host was shot for his kindness. North of Saint Quentin, at Le Catelet, another six men were discovered and similarly shot by firing squad.

Gradually such reminders of the British army's presence vanished as the invasion turned into an organised occupation. At first irritating, disturbing and uncomfortable, this complete take-over of French lives soon became more alarming. On Sunday 6 December 1914 all men between 18 and 39, some seven or eight hundred (many more were of course absent in the French army), were instructed to report to the barracks. After some four hours' waiting in the icy December weather they were directed to move off under German guard - destination unknown. Wives and mothers followed, weeping and calling out in their despair, answered by cries from the ranks of 'Goodbye Mother', while others began to sing the Marseillaise as the men departed. The families were left full of sadness, bitterness and anger.

Perhaps they were cheered four days later by the news - evidently censorship was not yet complete - that two German warships, the *Scharnhorst* and the *Gneisenau,* had been sunk by the Royal Navy in the Falkland Islands on 8 December.

New Year 1915 did not start well. The German authorities ordered the Mayor to provide three coffins: three French soldiers found in possession of military equipment were arrested that morning, and shot without trial. One had been denounced by his wife for concealing arms and ammunition, which was an accurate statement. The diarist who recorded this sad betrayal also noted that the woman was a drunkard and the mother of seven children by seven different fathers. Another French man, a retired soldier of over 60, reported that the two ancient rifles found in his house were mementoes picked up on the battlefield near Saint Quentin during the Franco-Prussian war, in 1871; the third, a railway official, was looking after his employer's house when German searchers found military equipment hidden in a tank - concealed there several months earlier and unknown to the caretaker. His explanation and pleadings were ignored.

The three men were lined up before a German firing squad in St.

German Firing Squad. Leutnant Hauss, in command of the firing squad, salutes the French men who have just been executed. Unfortunately one was not killed outright and Leutnant Hauss ordered the squad's NCO to administer the *coup de grâce.*

Hilaire barracks, blindfolded despite resistance on the part of the old soldier. With the front rank kneeling and the rear one standing, Leutnant Hauss gave the order to fire; but unfortunately, perhaps because of some reluctance to kill an old man, the veteran was not killed outright and the squad's sergeant-major was called forward to administer the *coup de grâce.*

Civilians found themselves stopped at random in the street, arrested as spies, condemned to a night or two in prison cells for any slight infringement of the increasingly onerous regulations. The whole city was constantly at risk of reprisals, for example following allegations that escaped prisoners were being hidden and that financial levies would follow any failure to give them up, or that the authorities would clear the schools and set the children to work in the fields.

Although the ordinary German soldier was very strictly disciplined, particularly over any incident involving drunkenness, with drinking establishments closely supervised, the officers benefited from a more relaxed approach. Residents with officers billetted in their houses recorded excessive drinking, with officers staggering down the stairs or damaging furniture and household fittings.

There was also the delicate matter of the young ladies who were attracted by the officers' uniforms and who accompanied the officers to the surviving places of entertainment. They were recognised as a danger and would denounce their fellow French citizens to the German authorities, always with dire consequences. These collaborators were recognised as exceptions to the rule, for the great majority of French women retained an air of dignity and reserve in the face of the various provocations.

Gradually, the atmosphere became one of oppression and terror for the inhabitants. Rural workers were treated like serfs and men and women ordered out from the city to work on the land were coerced by threats of prison or even shooting.

Buildings and amenities of all sizes and types were commandeered as the German administrative system took up residence in what was evidently recognised as an important centre. At 8 p.m. one evening the people of Saint Quentin heard tremendous cheering which later proved to be the German troops' response to the Kaiser, who under a strong guard made a tour of inspection of the city centre. It was the first of several such visits including the occasion when, in the presence of the Mayor, he inaugurated an impressive monument to the dead in the cemetery of Saint Martin, now the German military cemetery on the Chaussée Romaine. During the war this held the graves of French and

The Kaiser at the inauguration of the German Military Cemetery in Saint Quentin, 18 October 1915.

St. Martin Military Cemetery, Saint Quentin. During the fighting, the cemetery came under shellfire and the right-hand side of the monument was damaged. By the time of the liberation a total of 134 British dead had been buried here, but some of the graves had been lost. In the 1920s, when these British burials were re-interred in St Souplet CWGC cemetery, they were commemorated with an appropriate memorial.

Fire at Saint Quentin Station. In July 1916 an ammunition train was set on fire by British aircraft. This drawing shows the blaze as seen from south of the city.

British soldiers as well as Germans, the crosses giving the soldiers' name, home and age.

One of the many regulations was that all officers riding in their cars must be saluted as they passed through villages, on pain of possible arrest in case of failure. At least one ingenious Frenchman endeavoured to evade the humuliating requirements by pleading bad eyesight; he was sent to have his eyes tested and when the French optician naturally confirmed the 'defective' eyesight and prescribed spectacles, the victim was compelled to pay for them and wear them despite his perfect sight. He was not alone in this predicament.

Identity cards must be carried at all times, to be shown when required. The bread ration amount-

A modern view of the station.

ed to 185 grammes, less than a third of the pre-war average consumption, fishing, trapping or shooting game was forbidden - only the occupying forces could benefit from wild sources. Poaching naturally became widespread, regarded as an act of patriotism since it deprived the Germans of food.

Official house searches led to requisitions of all kinds of household goods and fittings, with imprisonment or forced labour in case of resistance. There were unofficial raids too, for it was not unusual to return home to find German soldiers armed with rifles ransacking the house, usually looking for wine or bicycles. Front doors must be kept unlocked and German soldiers had the right of entry at any time, for any reason.

From time to time there were executions of innocent people, such as the nine Frenchmen shot for alleged espionage. (The town hall was instructed to supply coffins.) In this case again the firing squad did not achieve a quick clean execution, for the German forces could not muster sufficient expert riflemen to ensure instant death. The dead men were transported on carts to the cemetery at St. Jean, with local people watching the procession and shouting out 'Vive la France'.

Ordinary life in Saint Quentin effectively ceased for, as happened

German supply column in the ruins of Saint Quentin during the war.

everywhere in occupied northern France, factories of all kinds were stripped of their plant, machinery and stocks; goods, fittings and equipment were despatched to Germany and the workers and owners were required to help the German authorities in this destruction of their livelihood and employment. Workers were left idle, but where possible many took to productive gardening in their own plots or outside the city.

The civilian population diminished in numbers. What were known to the Germans as 'useless mouths', mainly people too old or too frail to contribute to the war economy, were despatched via Switzerland to unoccupied France, cared for by the Red Cross once they left German-

The Hindenburg Line

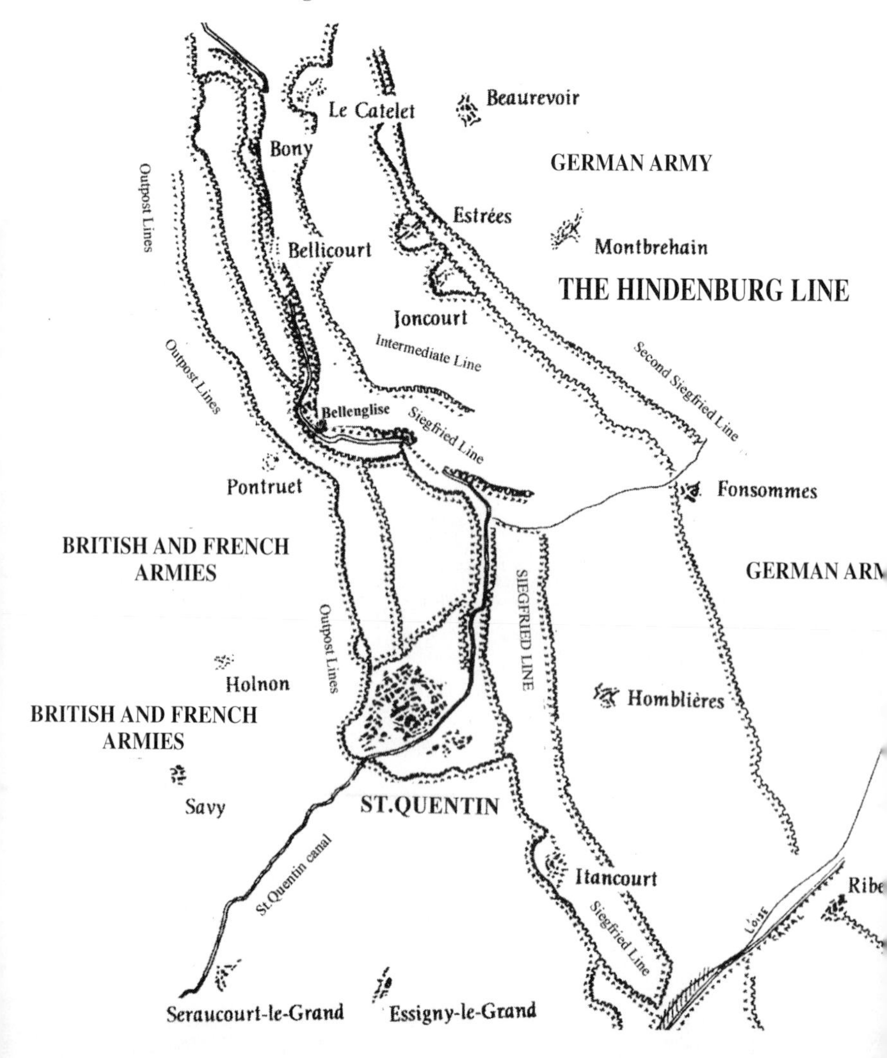

Civilians being evacuated: women, children and old men under German escort leaving Saint Quentin ahead of the German withdrawal to the Hindenburg Line.

controlled territory. Prostitutes suffering from venereal disease were also included in the group.

Although it lay well to the rear of the front line, Saint Quentin could be reached by air and French aircraft caused both considerable damage to war supplies and great rage among the occupying German army when they targeted the railway station area. Fuel tanks were hit by incendiary bombs, sending up great clouds of smoke and giving the people of Saint Quentin immense pleasure at the blow to their unwanted rulers. The consequence, not surprisingly, was that the streets were combed for muscle-power to repair the damage, and unlucky residents were press-ganged into clearing the railway tracks of debris so that the trains could run once more.

Realising that there would probably be more raids, the Germans made appropriate preparations and in a dawn raid by French aircraft a few days later one was badly damaged by artillery fire, forced to land, and the pilot, a captain, taken prisoner. The French aviators were not deterred, however, and continued to defy German anti-aircraft fire and fly over the city from time to time.

Despite censorship, news of battles filtered through to the inhabi-

Damaged buildings in the station district, possibly the result of explosions near the station caused by incendiary bombs dropped by French aircraft on German fuel tanks early in the occupation.

German defence posts (with branches on top as camouflage) near the city prison, commanding a good field of fire down the Boulevard Henri Martin. This strong-point at the corner of two open boulevards (Richelieu, Henri Martin) would have been difficult to overcome if the city had not been evacuated by German troops before the arrival of the French army on 1 October 1918.

tants. Expectations grew that the Allies would soon arrive and free them, but such anticipatory longings were quickly and cruelly destroyed over and over again.

In 1916 the artillery fire of the Battle of the Somme could be heard in the distance, and with great sadness the Saint Quentinois saw a train draw into the station with French prisoners from the fighting on the Somme, dejected and hungry, in a state of disarray. Any attempt at helping prisoners was severely punished, but some women succeeded in slipping money or food into their hands. At around the same time, all youths aged between 15 and 18 were summoned to register with the authorities; they must be prepared to be sent away from home to work in labour gangs.

By the end of 1916, however, the Germans were apparently already planning their retreat to the Hindenburg Line. This was the Allied name for what the Germans called the Siegfried Line, a defensive system of fortifications, several miles deep in some places, which was designed to present any attacking force with an impenetrable barrier.

Sections chosen as forward posts and various battle zones were protected by massive belts of barbed wire placed so as to funnel attackers into the concentrated fire of carefully sited machine-gun posts.

Residents of several villages lying to the west of Saint Quentin were given abrupt orders to pack up and leave immediately, some into the city and others to various towns in the region. The official German statement indicated that an offensive was expected from the French army in the spring, and the land was needed for the construction of strong-points and trenches. In fact the opposite was true, for the line was designed for the German army withdrawal, early in 1917, across terrain between Arras and the River Aisne. Large numbers of French labourers, in a state of effective slavery, left Saint Quentin under escort to work on Hindenburg Line constructions north of the city. Here they joined some 2,000 Russian prisoners who were making concrete dug-outs and laying out barbed wire entanglements. The Hague Convention rules that prisoners of war must not work on military construction were directly flouted.

These circumstances were known to the British at the time, through both aerial reconnaissance and escaped Russian prisoners. Further information came from the 'useless mouths' who were arriving in Switzerland from the occupied areas. Messages ordering certain German radio stations to prepare to move back were intercepted and the explosion of demolition charges at the transmitters heard, but the significance was not always understood by the Allies. As a result, the information was ignored and it was only on 25 February 1917, the day after the German withdrawal, that it was realised that the Hindenburg Line construction round Saint Quentin was fully traced by the Army.

At around the same time the civilians suffered further indignity and discomfort as their mattresses were requisitioned (the wool was required for German war purposes), coal became unobtainable, and municipal gas-lighting was only available for two hours in the late afternoon.

'A German soldier sees a Superior Officer': a sketch drawn and captioned by a French artist during the occupation. Carrying full equipment, rifle slung over his right shoulder and hand on rifle sling, the soldier appears to be acknowledging his officer with an 'eyes left'.

It was on 13 February 1917 that the villages round Saint Quentin were cleared. The old, the sick and the very young alike were turned out of their homes, families were broken up and the houses destroyed by dynamite charges. The buildings destroyed included the Château de Pommery, cottages in Fayet, and the church at Etreillers. Explosions continued on the outskirts of Saint Quentin, signalling the destruction of more buildings to enable a line of defence to be established to the west from north to south of the city. By the end of the month all civilians in these outlying areas had suffered forced evacuation. Fifty-five thousand people had been removed, some - knowing that their homes had been demolished and their land devastated - never to return. The city was never the same again after this loss of both inhabitants and their industrial or commercial livelihood, and it was not until 1954 that the population returned to its pre-1914 level.

The Germans were now established behind almost impregnable fortifications, ready to face the Allies without the encumbrance of non-combatants. The withdrawal to the Hindenburg Line was about to begin.

Chapter Four

THE HINDENBURG LINE

The German withdrawal in February 1917 to a specially prepared line was a dramatic event. The causes were simple in broad outline, for it was designed to economise on man-power and shorten lines of communication by at least 25 miles. There were German worries too, about the resilience of their troops. The Battle of the Somme had drawn deeply on their reserves of energy and General Ludendorff felt that his troops' offensive spirit could be restored quickly and effectively by simplifying and streamlining the military lay-out. In the meantime, unrestricted submarine warfare by the German navy during 1917 would be decisive.

A substantial slice of occupied France was given up but, as the advancing British discovered, the area was systematically devastated as part of the German withdrawal; many of the houses, farms and churches were demolished with explosive charges, trees were cut down and wells filled with rubbish and corpses. Able-bodied civilians were evacuated eastwards as part of the withdrawal but large numbers of old people, and small children with their mothers, were left behind as `useless mouths' and a hindrance to the German war effort. They were liberated by the advancing British troops, while French soldiers from the region hurried to their homes on leave and were horrified to find homes they had left in 1914 now rendered wholly unfit for habitation and aged relatives living in hovels.

The first inkling of the German withdrawal came on 24 February 1917 by a patrol of the 21st Manchesters (6th Manchester Pals) at Serre, on the Somme battlefield. (This was one of Manchester's many Pals battalions; the city quickly raised several thousand recruits through this system of encouraging, friends, neighbours or work colleagues to join up together with the promise that they would train and serve together. The system was abandoned after the bitter experience of many communities and families learning simultaneously of mass casualties, and recruits were usually no longer kept together.)

The first response to their report of the enemy leaving their trenches was that it `seemed almost incredible'; but the Manchesters' Commanding Officer, Colonel W. W. Norman, reported to Corps HQ that `I am of the opinion that it is reliable', and so indeed it was.

Moving into the area abandoned by the Germans was no simple matter as, withdrawing at their own pace, they made a stand when it suited them and fought strongly. The British inevitably suffered casualties and had to deal with polluted water supplies - a serious matter for the pursuing cavalry units - and 'crows' feet', devices designed to penetrate horses' hooves, were placed in the river bottom at every ford.

The German enthusiasm for this 'scorched earth' policy and for impeding the British advance overflowed into undisciplined behaviour, which was strongly deplored by the German High Command. The excessive acts of destruction, such as deliberately breaking up household utensils and burning furniture, were rightly seen as likely to give Germany a bad name. Perhaps the most prominent example was the widespread destruction wrought in Péronne where the retreating Germans left a large wooden sign attached to the Town Hall. With triumphal derision it proclaimed: 'Nicht ärgern, nür wundern!' ('Don't dispute, simply wonder!').[2]

The deliberate destruction along the route was occasionally of value to the advancing British, for the dynamited houses provided the troops with better shelter than the buildings which remained intact, obvious targets for German artillery. In addition, the ruins provided plenty of material to fill in the many craters blown by the enemy at strategic points along the roads.

The devastation left by the Germans was also, however, a drain on the Allies' manpower, as the troops were forced to undertake essential manual work. On 18 March, for example, all the infantry battalions of the 35th Division were ordered to halt their advance immediately and provide working parties to repair railways and roads. The Divisional artillery was attached to other divisions, including the 32nd in its pursuit of the Germans as they retreated to the outlying villages around Saint Quentin.

The 35th Division was originally formed as a 'Bantam' Division consisting of men standing between 5 feet and 5 feet 3 inches in height. The theory behind this was not always borne out by the practicalities; for although the original recruits were fit men who were simply below the usual height for enlistment, subsequent drafts and replacements proved unsuitable on other grounds. The Division was reorganised, and proved its worth later on.

This significant German withdrawal and British advance provided regimental diarists with the occasional amusing incident. One Midlands battalion, which took over from a French unit during the advance towards Saint Quentin, was instructed that they must speak in French when using the telephone for official communications. They complied - but it was quickly evident that any enemy listening in would

2. After many years in the Imperial War Museum, the notice was returned to Péronne and can now be seen in the Historial de la Grande Guerre.

Savy village during the German occupation: a German field artillery battery lined up outside Savy church. A small child in a white dress watches from the church doorway.

immediately realise, from the atrocious British accents, that the British had taken over. The order was rapidly cancelled.

On 18 March, the 1st and 3rd French Armies were ordered to follow the enemy to the Hindenburg Line, with the 1st and 3rd Cavalry Divisions instructed to open the route by preventing destruction along the way. They found their progress severely hindered by the mined bridges and crossroads and frequent traps; from time to time their advance was stopped by German snipers in ambush.

The German forces fell back steadily and reached Saint Quentin by 21 March 1917. A British instruction came through that day to make contact with the enemy and capture a German soldier 'dead or alive'.

Unusually, the task was given to a mounted patrol of the Royal Field Artillery. Led by a Battery Commander, it consisted of a further officer, the Battery Sergeant Major and six gunners. Major Lumsden, a staff officer from Brigade and shortly to win the Victoria Cross, completed the party. Entering the village of Savy, a village lying about three miles south-west of Saint Quentin, they engaged a German outpost where infantry were holding a crater near Savy railway station. Two of the defenders were wounded, the patrol galloped forward and captured one of them, who seemed to be only slightly hurt, while his comrade was

Savy railway station. A modern photograph of the disused station building. During the German retreat to the Hindenburg Line in March 1917 a mounted patrol (including Major Lumsden, who was shortly to win the V.C.) attacked an outpost beside the station and captured one of its defenders who was taken away for interrogation.

carried to safety. The patrol withdrew and the prisoner, who proved to be a non-commissioned-officer, was sent later that day under escort to 32nd Division headquarters near Nesle for interrogation.

The British reached Roupy on 31 March. From here they could see Savy, and Saint Quentin cathedral beyond. A dawn attack was scheduled for the next day; so a small party, this time from King Edward's Horse, was sent out on reconnaissance towards Savy. This type of reconnaissance in wartime might be undertaken by either cavalry or foot patrols, and appears to operate on a very simple basis, involving tentative moves towards the enemy who will then open fire and thereby indicate his position.

There was always a risk of casualties and on this occasion one of the party was shot from his horse; officers in Roupy, watching through binoculars, later saw German soldiers come out to the man and kick him. Satisfied that he was dead, they left him - but later still, under cover of darkness, the wounded trooper staggered back to the British lines, having successfully feigned death.

All was now set for the British forces to move forward next day and cap-

Roupy Village, view from the Chateau de Pommery. The battalions formed up along the road here before advancing across the field on the left, towards Savy.

ture Savy village - but by this time, the end of March 1917, the retreating Germans had decided to make a stand and engage in rearguard action at various locations in and around Saint Quentin. One of the selected sites where they intended to delay the British advance was a tactically strong position just in front of the new Hindenburg Line defences, on high ground about four miles to the west of Saint Quentin. It was here, between the villages of Savy and Holnon, that the enemy stood on the morning of 1 April 1917, ready to resist the advancing British.

The 15th & 16th Lancashire Fusiliers' attack on Savy, 1 April 1917. The picture looks along the line of attack: the two Battalions advanced as far as the railway embankment in the middle distance, which they took at the cost of over 200 casualties.

Savy village from the Roupy Road, a modern view across the field where the battalions advanced to take the village and the objectives beyond, including Manchester Hill. The Cross of Sacrifice in the village CWGC cemetery is visible on the edge of the village.

The strength of the German resistance was proved during the following fortnight, for it took the combined efforts of the 32nd, 61st and 35th Divisions and their battalions in various sectors around Saint Quentin to dislodge the German defenders, with many casualties on both sides.

The attack on Savy village was to be undertaken by two battalions from the 97th Brigade, 32nd Division, the 17th Highland Light Infantry ('The Glasgow Commercials') and the 11th Border Regiment ('The Lonsdales'). In 1914 Glasgow raised three battalions very quickly, the 15th H.L.I. known as the Glasgow Tramways Battalion, the 16th H.L.I. known as the Glasgow Boys' Brigade Battalion (each recruited from these sources) and the 17th H.L.I., based on the city's Chamber of Commerce. The 'Lonsdales' consisted of dalesmen from Cumberland and Westmorland, recruited by Lord Lonsdale and initially equipped at his own expense.

The French were asked to attack L'Epine de Dallon, lying to the east of Savy, for its capture would have been of great help to the British. However, they preferred to give artillery support to the attacking British. (It was only a month later that, with morale low and hopes of

Château de Pommery, a pre-war photograph. Blown up by the German army, its ruins later formed Goodman Redoubt, part of the defences held by the 17th Manchesters until they were driven out by the enemy on 22 March 1918 during the final German offensive

victory apparently fading, the first signs of mutiny began to appear in the French army. By this stage of the war, French losses had reached 1,300,000 dead and manpower was running short.)

During the night of 31 March 1917, the 17th Highland Light Infantry and the Lonsdales formed up on the road between the Château de Pommery and Roupy, then deployed into attack formation ready to advance towards Savy: it was a reverse of the scene in August 1914 when the British Army retreated through Roupy so hurriedly. The advancing troops, both British and French, looked forward to entering Saint Quentin. Civilians in the city had recently and forcibly been evacuated, removed further back behind the German lines.

The British artillery opened fire at 5 a.m. on 1 April 1917. Cover was provided by the guns of the 35th Division and the batteries moved successfully in daylight over open positions close to Savy. (This was a departure from usual practice and the authorities decided that artillery must be prepared in future to go into action over the open; from this time, guns would no longer be moved only under cover of darkness.) The two Battalions went into the attack on Savy village, keeping close behind the creeping barrage. Fighting was fierce in the streets, but

The post-war château photographed in 1999.

eventually the attackers killed or captured most of the German defenders. Next the village was put in an all-round state of defence, coming under heavy enemy artillery fire in the process.

The same two battalions were intended to continue and take the next objective, a wood between the village and the city known as Savy Wood. Reconnaissance patrols reported, however, that it was strongly held; it was decided that troops of 96 Brigade should be allocated to capture it, and the 15th and 16th Battalions of the Lancashire Fusiliers (the 1st and 2nd Salford Pals, raised in 1914 by Montague Barlow, Member of Parliament for South Salford) were called forward.

One of those left out was Corporal George Ashurst of the 16th Lancashire Fusiliers, a veteran who had joined up in 1914. On this occasion he was selected as Guard Commander at the Divisional General's headquarters in a château behind the lines. Ashurst, appreciating his good fortune in escaping the forthcoming battle, commiserated with a despondent sergeant friend who asserted that, 'It's my last trip'. His premonition was sadly accurate, for he was killed in his battalion's attack. Ashurst's account of the conversation does not name his friend, but the only sergeant in the 2nd Salford Pals to be killed on 1

April 1917 was No. 39468 Lance-Sergeant William Jones, a married man, who is buried in Savy British cemetery.

The attackers formed up some three miles from Savy Wood at the the Château de Pommery, so recently dynamited by the retreating Germans. At about 1 p.m. the Lancashire Fusilier battalions set off, the 15th battalion (1st Salford Pals) leading with the 16th (2nd Salford Pals) in the rear and the 16th Northumberland Fusiliers and 2nd Royal Inniskilling Fusiliers on the right. The 1st Salford Pals were to take the south-western corner of Savy Wood whilst at the same time swinging round to their right to capture the Halt (a railway junction with station and level crossing) on the Saint Quentin - Péronne railway line. The 2nd Salford Pals were to take the north end of the wood, to assist their sister battalion in mopping up, and thereafter form a reserve.

This meant advancing from the village of Savy north-eastwards across an open and gently rising slope with the Saint Quentin - Péronne railway line on a raised embankment, some 10-12 feet high, in front of them and crossing the fields at right angles to their line of attack. Beyond it lay a steeper slope with some rising ground known to the army as Round Hill. To their right lay two strongly-held machine-gun posts, one at a quarry (later called Manchester Quarry) and the other near The Halt railway junction.

The weather was appalling, with snow, hail, rain and a gale of wind throughout the day. In addition, the battalions suffered casualties on their way to Savy village - but by 4 p.m. the two Salford battalions had achieved the bulk of their objectives, with the exception of the quarry. It was not until 8.30 p.m., however, that the German machine guns at the Halt were silenced, when artillery fire was brought down on the position.

By the end of the day's action the supporting artillery batteries had fired 5,300 rounds of ammunition, but British casualties were heavy: 107 in the 15th Lancashire Fusiliers, the 1st Salford Pals and 124 in the 16th, the 2nd Salford Pals - including Ashurst's friend Sgt. Jones.

It was now the turn of 14 Brigade to continue the advance and at 5.0 a.m. on 2 April 1917 the four battalions in the Brigade moved forward to Savy Wood. The 15th H.L.I., on the right of the line, were charged with capturing the quarry, the 2nd Manchesters in the centre were to take the village of Francilly-Selency and the 1st Dorsetshire Regiment on the left of the line were responsible for taking the village of Holnon. The Brigade's remaining battalion, the 5th/6th Royal Scots, was held in reserve.

The Commanding Officer of the 2nd Manchesters was Lieutenant-

The Manchesters' attack on Savy Wood, 2 April 1917. Looking from the railway embankment, with Savy village behind the camera and Manchester Hill merging into Savy Wood on the right

Colonel Noel Luxmoore. In 1914 he was with the Devons, fighting on the Aisne, and was wounded at Vailly on 15 September. His return to active service took him to Hill 60, to attachment to the 2nd Manchesters - during which he was wounded again - and then to the Somme where he led the Battalion in their attack on the Leipzig salient on 1 July 1916. According to a sergeant serving with the 32nd Division's trench mortar batteries, Luxmoore was known as 'Corky' on account of his cork leg - presumably the result of one of his wounds.

Luxmoore was amused during the briefing that, despite the complex nature and obvious difficulty of the tasks to be undertaken, he was told that the closely neighbouring villages of Holnon and Francilly-Selency could be distinguished by their churches - one had a spire, the other a tower. As neither village had buildings standing more than 8 feet high by now, this was not particularly helpful! One important task was to be the capture of the Quarry (later known as Manchester Quarry) by the 15th H.L.I. Some 250 yards long by 150 yards wide, with steep sides into which the Germans had built dug-outs, it was very strongly held with machine-guns firing not only to the front but also to the sides.

The Manchesters moved up from billets in the village of Beauvois to Germaine, about 5 miles away, hoping for a rest; but were quickly required to rendezvous with others in the Brigade at the Château de Pommery, where a few trees and hedges marked the site of the former magnificent building. From the château near Roupy they set out for Savy, suffering some casualties under shell-fire from Saint Quentin.

One of these was 2nd Lieutenant Hubert Gaukroger, killed on 2 April near Roupy. His name is known to many students of literature of the First World War: one of his friends was another Second Lieutenant in the Manchesters, the poet Wilfred Owen. Gaukroger is buried in Savy British military cemetery.

The column passed through Savy village and over the open fields to halt behind the recently-captured Saint Quentin-Péronne railway embankment, resting while Lieutenant-Colonel Luxmoore went along the railway line to where the Highland Light Infantry were in position and ready to attack. Here he learned that the original plan had changed; the heavily-defended Quarry was now to be captured by the 2nd Manchesters instead of the H.L.I.

At dawn on 2 April the Manchesters began their attack under heavy rifle and machine-gun fire, most of it from the Quarry. Two platoons were able to change direction slightly, however, and their successful assault on this strong-point captured four enemy machine-guns as well as others seized when they stormed a nearby trench. Next they pushed on towards Saint Quentin, until they were brought up short by a very large crater on its outskirts. Urgent messages to Battalion HQ asked for support, but without response; by nightfall they were forced to withdraw, and the opportunity to advance further into the city was lost.

Meanwhile the rest of the battalion was moving forward. Open grass-land lay beyond the raised railway embankment running across the battlefield, rising gently for about three-quarters of a mile to Francilly-Selency before a shallow dip and another fairly steep rise to Selency - the village which was the Manchesters' final objective.

Suddenly, they came across a German battery of 77 mm guns, lying on low ground to the south-east of the village. Two companies attacked the battery from two sides and, after a hand-to-hand fight with some of the gunners who had not fled, captured all six guns. A small party remained with the battery while the remainder continued the advance beyond Francilly-Selency, finally taking Selency village some 90 minutes after leaving the railway embankment.

The 15th H.L.I., following up with the 2nd Manchesters, had few casualties, but as they joined the exhausted and depleted Manchesters in Francillly they came under heavy shell fire and suffered 40 casualties while they rapidly dug a series of trenches in the newly-won ground. Here as elsewhere throughout the British Army, among the responsibilities of one of the Divisional Padres, the Revd. R. E. Grice-Hutchinson, was to bury the dead whenever possible. It was particularly important to mark and record the graves; this he did by drawing a number of pegs from the Corps chaplain which he placed over the graves as he visited the burial sites.

(After the war, the battalion history of the Highland Light Infantry refers to the 2nd Manchesters, whose regimental HQ was in north-west England, as 'the Midland battalion'. To a Scottish regiment based in Glasgow, Manchester and Salford were so far south as to qualify as 'the Midlands'.)

Although the Manchesters took heavy casualties as they stormed forwards, the 1st Dorsets, like the 15th H.L.I. had very few casualties and captured Holnon quite easily before moving on to their final objective, the main Saint Quentin road.

The only outstanding matter was the group of six German field guns captured by the Manchesters, guarded by a small escort from the battalion. The Germans could be expected to counter-attack from the outskirts of Saint Quentin at any moment, and the exhausted Manchesters were in no shape either to repulse an attack or to bring in the guns.

This task was allocated to the 15th Highland Light Infantry.

British Bombardment on St Quentin.

Chapter Five

BRINGING IN THE GUNS

The battery of six 77 mm guns was clearly the 2nd Manchesters' treasure trove and despite their weariness and casualties they had tried to bring them in during the night of their capture, 2 April. The attempt had failed, through shortage of men and lack of suitable drag-ropes. They then retired to trench lines facing Saint Quentin from where they could fire on any German effort to recover their weapons.

The 15th Highland Light Infantry (Glasgow Tramways Battalion) were later ordered to bring in the guns. The hauling party was selected from the Battalion's strongest men and it was eventually a party of one officer and thirty men which left Savy Wood under the command of Major F. W. Lumsden, Royal Marine Artillery. As they made their way into No Man's Land near Francilly Selency a covering party moved into position about 1,000 yards south-east of the village.

Instructed not to enter the battery position, because it was believed that a German soldier had been left there to give the alarm over the battery's cable to German HQ in the city, they were in position by 8.15 p.m. on 3 April. An eye-witness describes how `the water tower and cathedral spire were touched with silver' by the moonlight.

The tense silence of the night was broken almost immediately, for the German artillery laid a brief barrage of fire round the disputed battery. Next the covering party came under attack from a large force of German 'sturmtruppen', about 100 men, making for the battery, for both British and Germans had decided at the same time to send out parties to bring in the guns. German shouts of 'H.L.I.' were designed to create confusion, but eventually they were driven off, leaving two officers and twelve men dead. (The officers carried no badges of rank but wore white gloves as a means of identification.)

Meanwhile, the hauling party reached the guns without casualties. The first one was manhandled over very rough ground, almost turning over, but was taken to the British lines where teams of horses were waiting under the command of Captain Ward of 161 Brigade Royal Field Artillery. Through intense and wearying labour and often under fire, the thirty men managed to bring in a further four guns but the sixth artillery piece, damaged by shell-fire, was stuck in a trench. Despite their exhaustion the hauling party, with horses, managed to lift it out of the trench by sheer strength.

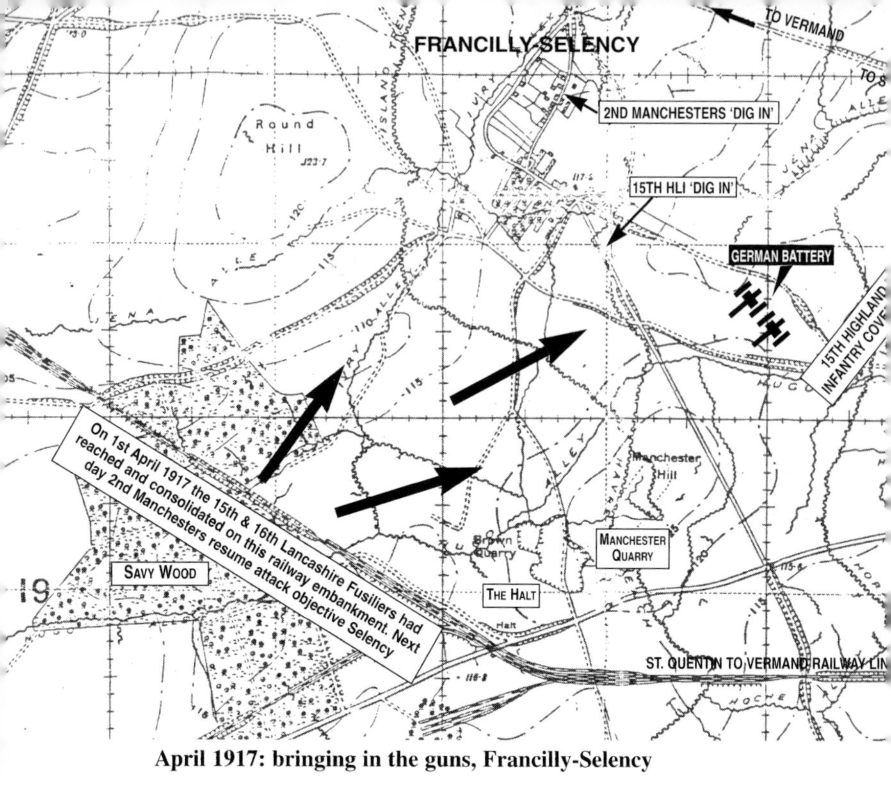

April 1917: bringing in the guns, Francilly-Selency

Worn out, they could no longer carry on; Major Lumsden sent them back to rest and collected another party of men to bring in this last gun in the German battery. Its recovery was not essential - but it was a matter of pride. A German raiding party took advantage of the interval before the second party reached it and blew in the breech of the already damaged gun, but it was retrieved and by 1 a.m. on 4 April 1917 the operation was successfully completed.

Casualties were not light. 2nd Lieutenant J. V. Johnston was killed, and thirty Other Ranks were wounded or missing. Major Lumsden was awarded the Victoria Cross, and within a few days received meteoric promotion to Brigadier-General in command of 14 Brigade. Lieutenant Calderwood, who had led the hauling party, was awarded the Military Cross.

It was the first time that a complete enemy battery had been taken, and the 2nd Manchester were, with justification, extremely proud of the exploit. In Savy Wood close by, Wilfred Owen, who arrived too late to share in the attack, wrote home to his mother with regimental pride after seeing the guns brought in: 'We captured six guns . . .'

Hitherto the French had not felt able to contribute infantry in support of the British attacks of 1 April, but with the capture of Savy and

Selency now confirmed it was clear that a successful advance on the French front without heavy casualties was much more probable. On the afternoon of 4 April, therefore, in a tremendous snow storm, a picked battalion of French troops advanced from the trenches held by the 16th H.L.I. at Roupy. They attacked and captured the village of L'Epine de Dallon and patrols reached Rocourt, a suburb of Saint Quentin, taking a number of prisoners. 'A great sight to see the blue lines go forward and it cheered us no end to know they were succeeding', was the comment by an observer. There was swift German retaliation. Men of the 16th H.L.I. came under fire in Roupy Quarry, a position well known to the German artillery, and in the space of a few minutes one officer had been killed, three wounded (including the Medical Officer, whose foot was blown off) and 26 Other Ranks wounded. Two R.E. sappers who had been timbering the walls in a cellar were also killed.

Some time later a regular soldier in the Royal Dublin Fusiliers appeared in the battalion orderly room with a highly-coloured story of trying to give help and first aid to the men who had been near the Quarry at the time of the shelling. He was really asking the C.O. for a recommendation for the Victoria Cross, feeling that the subsequent public subscription for his courage and the accompanying cash award would be a useful addition to his army pension when he returned home to Ireland. The Commanding Officer interviewed the man and sent him on his way - determined that if the man did acquire a farm it would not be through such an ingenious invention.

What was to be done with the captured German 77 mm guns? Six were available for British use: the 2nd Manchesters were given two and the 15th H.L.I. took over a single gun. The help given by 159 Brigade Royal Field Artillery, in assisting with their wagons, entitled them to another three. One of the enemy guns left in working order was handed over to the Trench Mortar Battery of the 32nd Division.

As ever, the French were determined that Saint Quentin should not be shelled. They were particularly anxious that the cathedral should not be damaged in any way, despite the obvious value of the spire to the Germans as a fine observation-point. The men of the 32nd Division Trench Mortar Battery were evidently not aware of this French concern, for on 8 April they decided to bring their German gun into action. They had received about 100 rounds of ammunition and, taking careful aim on the spire of Saint Quentin cathedral, hit it with their first shot - no doubt upsetting the French but eliminating the German observation post. The observation platform, however, was promptly installed in a neighbouring belfry tower.

On the same day, Easter Sunday 1917, the Divisional Padre was taking a service in Holnon Wood. Over to the French sector south-east of Saint Quentin an observation balloon was visible, under attack by a German fighter plane. Just before the balloon burst into flames the observer took to his parachute and floated down to earth, landing safely within the French lines. Two French scout planes immediately engaged the German aircraft, sending it crashing into a field near Villevecque some 300 yards from the padre and his morning service.

A description of the incident and the German crash survives in one of Wilfred Owen's letters. The 2nd Manchesters were out of the line, resting in cellars in the ruins of Beauvois village not far from Villevecque; Owen heard the crash and went in search of souvenirs. Writing to his brother, he identifies the aircraft as a new Albatros, No. 2234. He took the dead pilot's handkerchief as a souvenir.

These attacks on 1-2 April 1917 on Savy and beyond by the 32nd Division were not undertaken in isolation.

The 61st Division was also involved near Saint Quentin, part of a 'pincer' movement designed to encircle the city. Its task was to pursue the enemy by operating from the Vermand area, north-west of the activities at Savy. Its orders included attacks towards Bihecourt, on the north side of the River Omignon, and Maissemy on the opposite bank.

One of the battalions to be involved in these operations was the 2/5th Gloucestershire Regiment. It included the composer and poet Private Ivor Gurney, who served on the Somme, at Arras, Ypres and Passchendaele and whose tragic life ended with his death in an asylum in December 1937, where he had lived for some twelve years. He was wounded at Bihecourt on 7-8 April 1917 and subsequently gassed in the Ypres Salient. Gurney was the antithesis of the smart soldier, but the Glosters' RSM was inclined to overlook his inadequacies, remarking on one occasion to the CO that Gurney was 'a good man, sir, but he's a musician'.

The village of Vermand lies about $3\frac{1}{2}$ miles west of Saint Quentin by a bridge over the River Omignon, on the great Roman road to Amiens (it was indeed originally a Roman settlement and is proud of its ancient history). In the opening weeks of the war - on 27 August 1914 - some British battalions passed through Vermand on their retreat to the Marne; but now, as units of the 61st Division arrived on 31 March 1917, the empty village presented a very different picture and bore all the familiar signs of devastation left by the Germans in their withdrawal to Saint Quentin and the Hindenburg Line.

During the German retreat to the Hindenburg Line the Royal Flying

Corps acted as messenger, keeping the British troops in touch. German air activity was virtually non-existent in this area; knowing that they were liable to come under attack from the British in the Arras sector and the French in Champagne, they concentrated their air forces in these two areas. (The RFC nickname of 'Bloody April' referred to their heavy losses around Arras that month, many of them involving aircraft escorting the slower-moving reconnaissance aeroplanes sent out to take photographs of the Hindenburg Line and beyond. RFC units monitoring the retreat to Saint Quentin were therefore generally unimpeded.)

There were victims in the air, however. One of these was Second Lieutenant N.A.Phillips, a fighter pilot of No.54 Squadron which was involved in a dog-fight over Saint Quentin on 25 March 1917 with the German Jasta 20 fighter squadron. Shot down to the south-west of the city, he died in the crash and is buried in Grand Seraucourt British Cemetery not far from Roupy.

The Saint Quentin-Péronne railway line crossed the Roman road and the River Omignon here in Vermand, with a station on the Vermand-Bihecourt road. Beyond the road by the station the railway track followed an embankment and it was here, at this good tactical position, that the 2/5th Glosters dug in on their arrival on 31 March. Some German cavalry - Uhlans - were visible skirmishing in Holnon Wood not far away. (The wood was finally captured by the 1st Dorsets on 2 April 1917.)

The night of 31 March - 1 April was bright and cold. A patrol of Glosters was despatched to discover whether Bihecourt was occupied; approaching the village, one man sneezed and the patrol was immediately spotted and fired on, indicating that Bihecourt was indeed in enemy hands. On 2 April, however, while not far away the Manchesters, Dorsets and H.L.I. were attacking Francilly-Selency and Holnon Wood, the Glosters advanced the three-quarters of a mile of road to Bihecourt, captured it and passed on through to consolidate in the orchard beyond. (It was after this attack that Ivor Gurney wrote to a friend that the Division had been mentioned in despatches. Showing feelings perhaps unexpected in such an 'unsoldierly soldier', he remarked that 'we have risen a little in our own estimation . . . one does not wish to belong to a washout division'.)

The airspace above Saint Quentin offered occasional dramatic action, particularly for flyers from overseas. On 5 April the Australian 'ace' Major Dallas shot down a German Albatros two miles east of Saint Quentin, while on the next day the New Zealand Flight Sub

Lieutenant Culling of Naval I Squadron destroyed a German two-seater just north of the city. Another Albatros was shot down that day on the outskirts of the city by a Canadian, Captain Clement, M.C., of No.22 Squadron.

On the ground, meanwhile, the 2/8th Bn Worcestershire Regiment advanced to Villevecque (south of Vermand), then moved on to make contact with the Dorsets near Holnon Wood before continuing to Maissemy, just across the Omignon from the newly-captured Bihecourt. Preparations were now in hand for further advances towards the Hindenburg Line, and French pilots were busy observing the Germans lines and assessing the strength of their defences.

The Glosters' next attack, on 7 April, was a costly one on the German rearguard positions near Bihecourt. One of the nearly fifty casualties was Gurney, who was wounded in the arm. Next day, Easter Sunday, was spent in rest at Vermand, where they remained until relieved by the 35th Division in their continuing encirclement of Saint Quentin.

It was about this time that in a letter home Gurney wrote of a visit by most of the surviving company to the grave of one of the battalion's 'much-loved corporals'. Having served originally with a Northern Cyclist battalion, he was killed in action on 5 March 1917 in the Ablaincourt sector. The Germans who buried him placed a simple wooden cross on his grave, with the inscription, 'Hier ruht ein tapfere Engländer' ('Here lies a brave English man . . .'). His English friends were struck by the contrast between this German chivalry and the total destruction wrought during their retreat to Saint Quentin.

The attacks resumed a few days later, on 13 April 1917, when the French asked for a British attack on the village of Fayet, to the north-west of Saint Quentin and overlooking it. This was to coincide with an attack by units of the Third French Army in their own sector to the south of the city and although General Rawlinson was initially reluctant, preferring to wait until the success of the French attack became clearer, instructions were never the less issued for the 2nd King's Own Yorkshire Light Infantry and the 16th H.L.I. to be prepared to make the assault when ordered, with the 11th Borders (Lonsdales) in reserve (32nd Division).

The proposed French attack on 13 April reflected the desire of the French army's General Humbert to begin an attack on the Hindenburg Line and, if possible, to enter Saint Quentin itself. His orders, promulgated on 4 April, emphasised the importance of avoiding damage to the city and its railways.

It was to be a two-pronged attack; the first was directed at a line

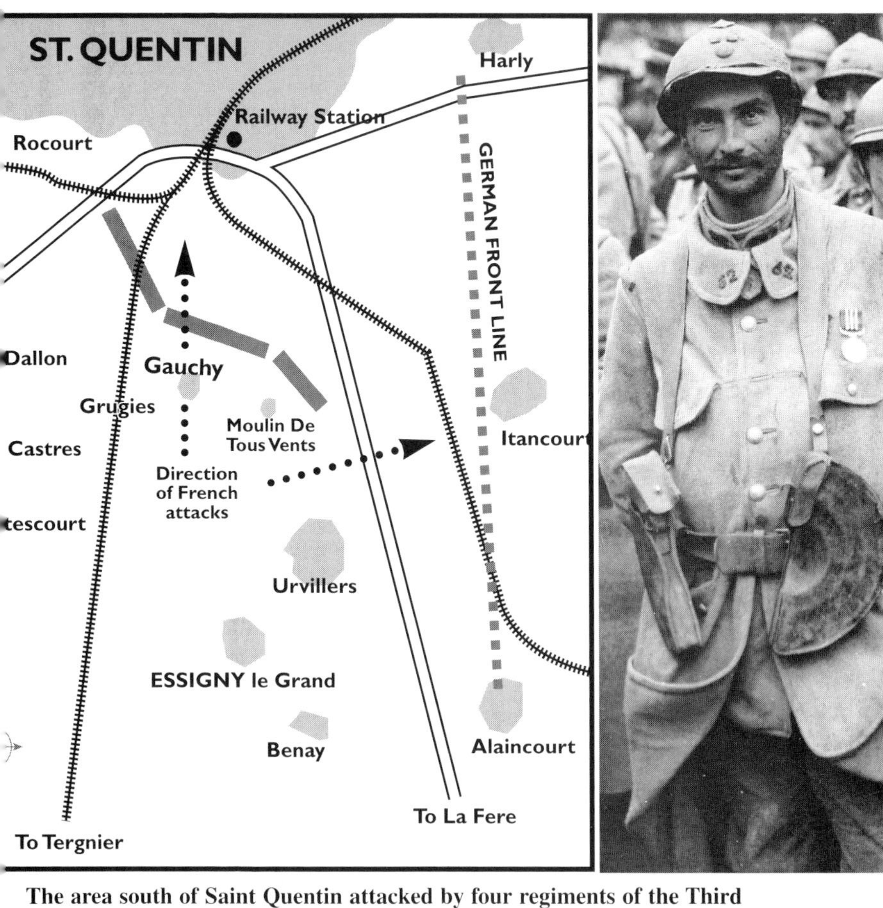

The area south of Saint Quentin attacked by four regiments of the Third French Army, 13 April 1917.

The Post-war ruins of Grugies church. Forming part of the outer defences of the Hindenburg Line south of Saint Quentin, the church had been destroyed and used as a German defence post and shelter. Two regiments of the French army were involved in an attack at Moulin de Tous Vents just north of this village on 13 April 1917.

drawn eastwards from the Saint Quentin suburb of Rocourt to a mill, the Moulin de Tous Vents, with the line running just north of Gauchy and, on the edge of Saint Quentin itself, about a kilometre from the railway station. At the same time the second part was to be a French attack on part of the German front line on the east of Saint Quentin, running southwards between Harly and Ablaincourt.

Four French regiments, about 6,000 men, went into action at 5 a.m. on 13 April. Despite every effort and bitter fighting, they were unsuccessful in the Gauchy area, but made better progress to the east. The

The British attacks on 14 April 1917 - outline of events. At 4.30 a.m. the 2nd K.O.Y.L.I, 16th H.L.I. and later the 11th Borders commenced the assault on the Fayet area and beyond. By 2 p.m. they were established not far from Gricourt, on the Gricourt - Saint Quentin road. At 6.30 a.m. the 1st Dorsets attacked Cepy Farm, and by 9 a.m. had captured the farm and established a line stretching south and facing Saint Quentin. Some time after 2 p.m. the 2nd Manchesters attacked and took Dancour Trench, which was found to be empty. At 8.30 p.m. the 5th Royal Scots took over and the Manchesters returned to Savy Wood.

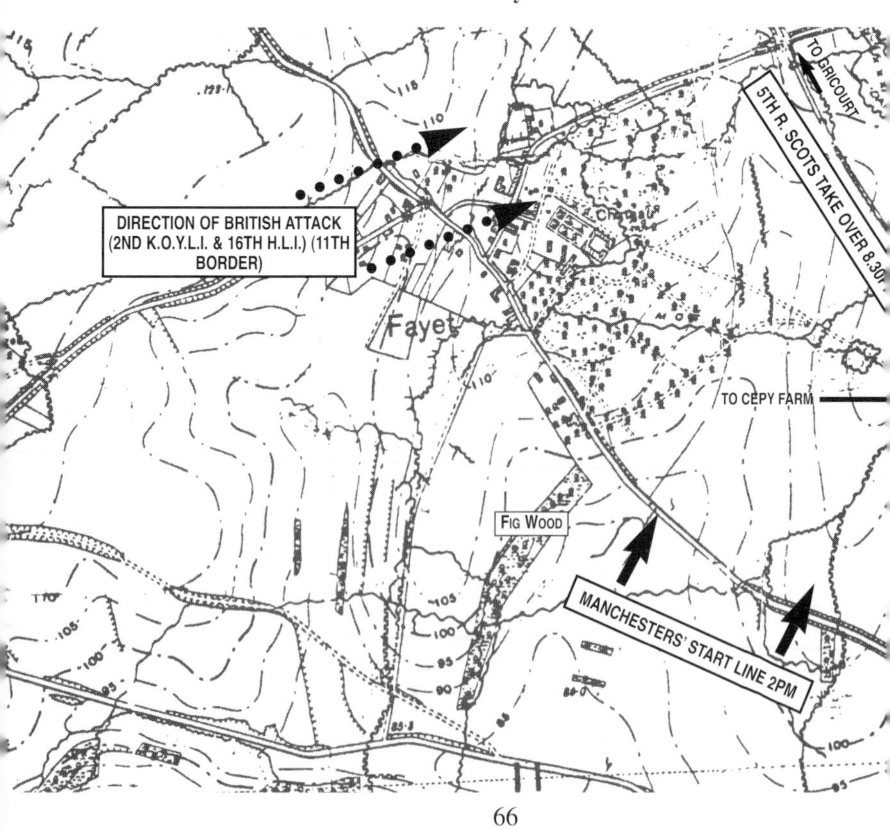

German front line, astride the Saint Quentin - La Fère road, was captured at a cost of some 1,600 casualties. A number of factors contributed to the failures: barbed wire had not been destroyed beforehand, the German machine-guns were well-sited and concealed, often in blockhouses - and every movement was clearly observed from the city itself. Finally, the German artillery batteries sited near the railway station and in the Place de l'Hôtel de Ville caused many French casualties.

At 4.30 a.m. next day, 14 April, the British began their assault, designed to achieve an advance in the Fayet area towards the Saint Quentin-Gricourt road. In their first rush the 2nd K.O.Y.L.I. and 16th H.L.I. captured some 100 German soldiers, but a feature called the Twin Copses just beyond Fayet proved difficult to take. By 1 p.m. the 11th Borders, in reserve, were on the move under orders to seize the position. Despite casualties, they were successful about twenty minutes later and established contact with the 16th H.L.I. to the north, towards Gricourt, by 2 p.m.

The 16th H.L.I. had hastened through the skirmishing in Fayet village, captured Fayet château after some initial confusion, and then pressed on towards the Gricourt road. The Battalion was delighted with this achievement, since they were not expected to make the capture for another 1½ hours. The success of these battalions gave valuable support to the 1st Dorsets in their task of holding the Cepy Farm line facing Saint Quentin and also to the imminent attack by the 2nd Manchesters.

The relative ease with which Fayet and its immediate area was taken was the result of several factors, one of which was the element of surprise and the efficiency of the British artillery. Another was the bewildered state of the defending German troops; most of them were young men from the borders of Russia, pressed into service by Germany because of a decline in man-power. (From mid-1915 on, the German army had already been forced to restructure its divisions gradually, with fewer units in each) The battle was not without cost, however, with the 16th H.L.I., for example, suffering some 140 casualties before taking the final objective.

In the captured German billets the men of the H.L.I. discovered that the young soldiers, disconcerted by the surprise attack, had abandoned their recently-issued new boots and underwear. A few of the H.L.I. could not resist discarding their own badly-worn footwear and adopting the German boots: but at the next company kit inspection they suffered by having their pay docked for failing to produce regulation

Saint Quentin Cathedral: a war-time view from Cepy Road, close to Dancour Trench.

Army boots. Another Scottish soldier was seen to throw away his lice-infested vest and replace it with a fresh clean one from a German pack.

All was now ready for an attack by the 2nd Manchesters. Fayet was in British hands and the line of their impending assault north-eastwards was secured on the flanks, on one side by the 11th Borders (Lonsdales) and the 16th H.L.I. towards the Gricourt area and on the other by a line established earlier by the 1st Dorsets on the outskirts of Saint Quentin, ending at Cepy Farm. The Dorsets were justifiably proud of their battalion's early morning attack on Cepy Farm, for it had an influence on the Lonsdales' eventual capture of Twin Copses. Reaching the farm involved crossing some 600 yards of open ground under continuous fire but, unwavering despite many casualties, the extended line of men advanced steadily under fire from enemy troops in the farm which only ceased as they came within 50 yards of the farmyard gate. At this point the German garrison fled. It was just 9.00 a.m.

The 2nd Manchesters were ordered to attack a position known as Dancour Trench north-west of Saint Quentin, further along the road past Cepy Farm and parallel with the Saint Quentin-Gricourt road. The logical route to reach the attack start line, on the edge of Saint Quentin, would seem to be at a small wood called Bois des Roses, near Francilly-Selency and on the Amiens-Saint Quentin road - but Lieutenant-Colonel Luxmoore, the Commanding Officer, realised that to move through here would bring the battalion under devastating fire from Saint Quentin and its Hindenburg Line. The route that he therefore selected involved a circuitous diversion to the west of Selency, to a more sheltered site near the flank cover provided by the Dorsets' recent capture of Cepy Farm.

The 2nd Manchesters left Savy Wood in the mid-morning of 14 April, stopped short of the Bois des Roses position and looped back round to the west of Selency (possibly following the route of the old Roman road which still exists as a field track on the modern map) before bearing north across the modern N.29 Amiens-Saint Quentin road. Crossing the flat fields they were out of enemy view, and after

Fayet-Squash Valley. The 2nd Manchesters rested here around mid-day on 14 April 1917 on their circuitous route from Savy Wood to the attack start-line on the edge of Saint Quentin. Fayet village and château had just been captured and the way was now clear for the battalion to move up this slope, over the clear hill-crest and down through Fig Wood on the far side to the assembly point before the uphill attack on Dancour Trench. During the descent to the assembly point the battalion, now well within range of the enemy guns, came under intense fire from German artillery in Saint Quentin and took heavy casualties.

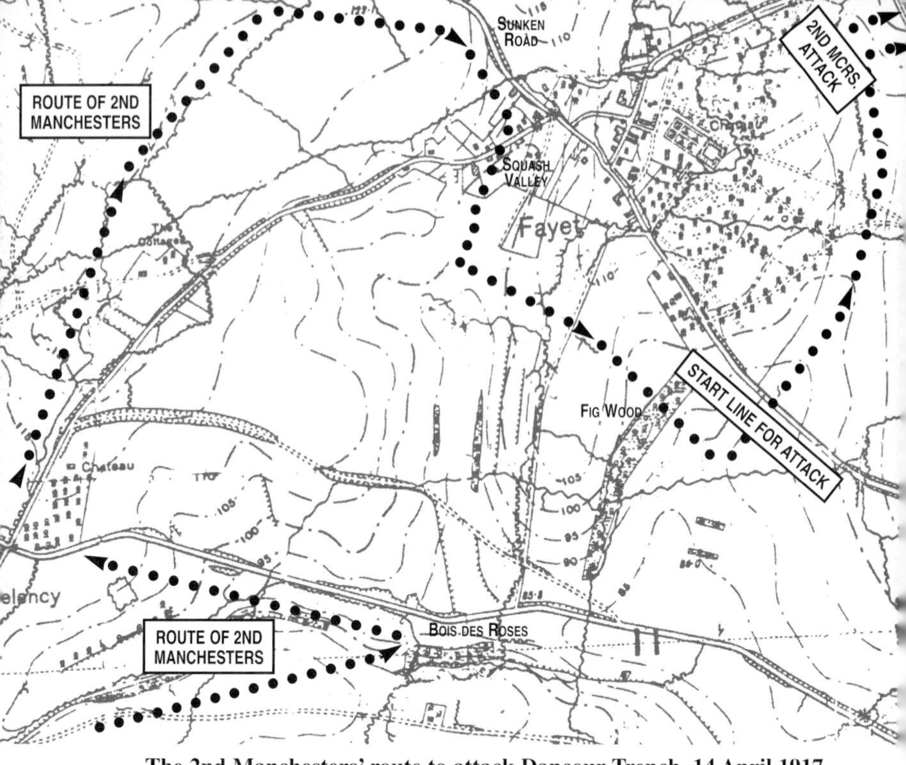

The 2nd Manchesters' route to attack Dancour Trench, 14 April 1917.

following a sunken road into Fayet village and branching off to the right they halted in a dip known to the British as Squash Valley.

The pause here was a brief moment of peace, for with the now-imminent capture of Twin Copses it was almost time for the battalion to move off. Their next manoeuvre would take them up on to a narrow ridge, down the other side and into a copse, Fig Wood, before assembling for the assault on Dancour Trench. It was just after mid-day when orders were given to cross the ridge, where the Manchesters immediately came into view of the Germans in Saint Quentin; heavy fire caused around thirty casualties as the Battalion hurried down through Fig Wood to a position spot south of Fayet village, where they formed up for their attack.

The 2nd Manchesters' advance from here lay up a fairly steep valley slope, with a sharp turn to the right at the top to achieve a frontal approach to Dancour Trench. Protected on their right flank by the 1st Dorsets' recent capture of the Cepy Farm line, they moved off at 2.30 p.m. - and as they advanced, were caught from behind by rifle fire from a few enemy troops in a wood nearby on their left - but they were promptly dealt with by 'moppers up' following behind. To the British troops' surprise, the trench was empty when they reached it, the

The view from Dancour Trench. A modern view from the site of Dancour Trench, captured by the 2nd Manchesters on 14 April 1917. Their assembly point was at the present-day location of the white buildings (centre), before advancing up the slope towards the camera position. The 1st Dorsets were holding a flank trench outpost line to the left of this view, and as the Manchesters advanced they came under sporadic fire from the wood in Fayet, visible to the right. The city of Saint Quentin is off to the left from this view.

inhabitants having fled precipitately. Later, after being relieved by the 5th Royal Scots, the Battalion returned to Savy Wood in calmer conditions.

The Germans were not, however, prepared to leave matters in this state, and on 15 April the 1st Dorsets in Cepy Farm came under heavy German artillery shelling, lasting from dawn till dusk and reportedly causing over a hundred casualties. One diarist - himself an artillery officer - commented on the large number of casualties. Writing later, he pointed out that Cepy Farm was a large isolated farmhouse with out-houses, a perfect target for enemy guns, and criticised the Dorsets' decision to remain in occupation after the capture.

Earlier, on 9 April, the 35th Division was ordered to move east from their uncongenial repair labour in the devastated regions. They were to take over from the 61st Division in the area of Bihecourt, Maissemy, Fresnoy-le-Petit, The Tumulus and Berthaucourt. The 35th Division had recently been completely reorganised and was ready for the next challenge, to go into action on 15 April 1917.

While the men of the Manchesters, Lonsdales, H.L.I. and others of

The Cathedral from Dancour Trench and the cathedral spire, destroyed by 32 Division gunners in April 1917 and later replaced.

the 32nd Division were in action around Fayet and the outskirts of Saint Quentin on 14 April, the 35th Division moved up and sent patrols of the 17th Lancashire Fusiliers forward towards Gricourt, which had been shelled during the 32nd Division attacks.

The patrols overcame strenuous opposition with intensive battalion mortar support, and took 45 prisoners; then, seeing German troops retreating, the Lancashire Fusiliers advanced and took the village at the cost of 44 casualties.

The battalion Lewis gunners then brought down an enemy aircraft that was attacking them - an unprecedented achievement which brought them high praise.

A strongly earth-bound challenge awaited them next, a farm known as Les Trois Sauvages east of Gricourt. As a tactically strong position it was to be defended fiercely - and successfully, for it never succumbed to the many British attacks.

The first of these onslaughts came from the 18th Bn Lancashire Fusiliers on 15 April 1917. Although they inflicted some 100 casualties in the hand-to-hand fighting, they were forced to withdraw under heavy machine-gun fire. Next day, an artillery spotting aircraft was badly damaged by German anti-aircraft fire from the city. Although the pilot managed to reach the British lines, the plane crashed at Savy, wounding the pilot and killing the observer, Second Lieutenant C.E.Wilson.

Ten days later, the airborne activity over Saint Quentin led to an unusual incident that involved four friends of Captain Clement (No.22 Squadron) at the highest governmental and diplomatic level. Two British aircraft, engaged in dropping propaganda leaflets over the German lines, were attacked and forced down in German-held territory. The four aircrew (Acting Captain Hawkins and Second Lieutenants McEntee, Hopkins and Stewart) were captured and - accused of disseminating inflammatory propaganda - were brought before a Court Martial. The court, however, considered that the charge was unjustified, and acquitted all four men. They were sent to a regular prisoner of war camp, while notice was given that any future aircrew found in possession of propaganda material would be dealt with severely.

Two more RFC officers were shot down and captured on a similar expedition on the day of the court's verdict, and a further pair were charged with the same offence later in the year; it required neutral protests to the German authorities (from the Netherlands) before the officers could be redirected to an ordinary prisoner-of-war camp for officers. The consequence was that future British propaganda leaflets would only be dropped from balloons and all air crews were now informed in writing that they must not carry printed or written propaganda material (an order that was maintained until the final days of the war).

While these aircraft were in action around and above Saint Quentin, the pattern of enemy machine-guns forcing the British ground forces to withdraw developed in every assault on the stronghold of Les Trois Sauvages; the 16th Cheshires tried their best to capture it over several days towards the end of April, followed by the 17th West Yorkshires on 3 May and the 19th Durham Light Infantry two days later, and then the 15th Sherwood Foresters on 9 May. On this occasion, the very heavy British artillery support combined with similar bombardment from the German artillery merely achieved the virtual demolition of the farm. Like their predecessors, the Foresters were finally forced to withdraw and, also like their predecessors, suffered casualties in the operation.

The whole situation was reviewed the next day and the Corps Commander's new orders instructed that although the farm could be raided it was not to be captured and held; perhaps rather late in the day,

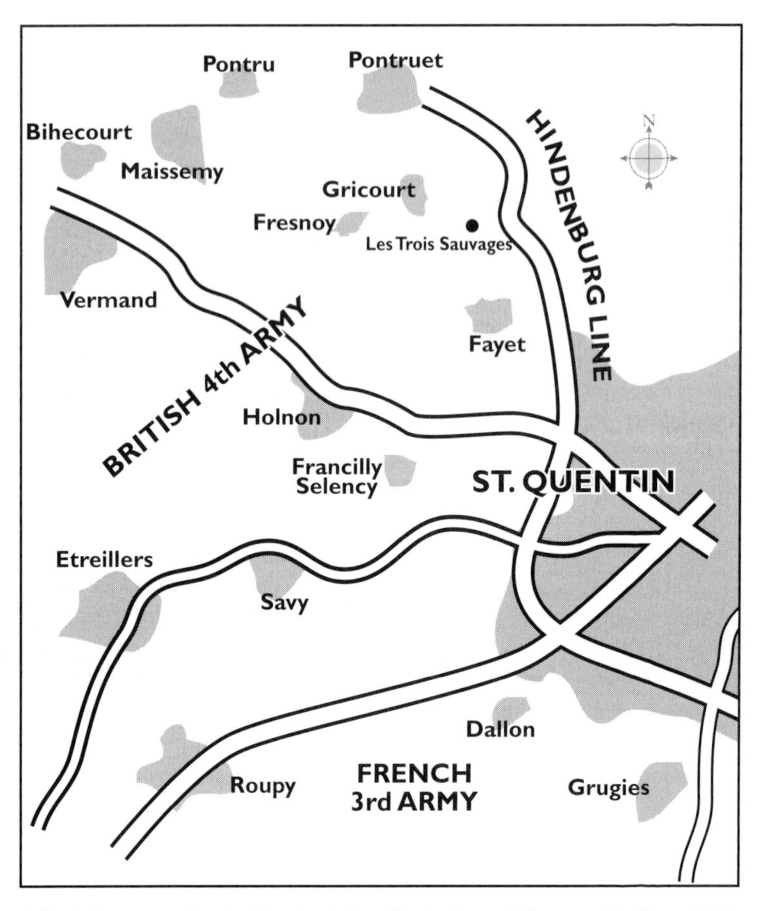

Allied forces arrive in front of the Hindenburg Line on 15 May 1917. Successful attacks by the 61st and 35th Divisions have driven the enemy back from Bihecourt, Maissemy and Pontru to Les Trois Sauvages. Savy, Holnon and Fayet have fallen to the 32nd Division and the French have forced the Germans back to the city suburbs. With the British required elsewhere, the French XI Corps took over the front five days later.

it was noted that occupying Les Trois Sauvages involved possession of a dangerous salient which would not justify the loss of life involved.

None the less, the Germans were not to be allowed to retain possession undisturbed; their habit of leaving the farm at dawn each day provided a good opportunity and on 13 May a dawn bombardment by a British battery, supported by the machine-guns of the 14th Bn Gloucestershire Regiment, inflicted some fifty enemy casualties. Two

In May 1917 the British army in front of Saint Quentin, handed over to the French army. Here, a French soldier watches from a sandbagged emplacement on the outskirts of the village.

days later the 15th Sherwood Foresters attacked the farm again, supported by mortar and machine-gun fire - but impenetrable barbed wire forced them to retreat at the cost of around 40 casualties.

Next it was the 14th Glosters who took over. One of their men, Private Blick, crawled out to some of the wounded men lying between the farm and an outpost, and managed to rescue two of the Sherwood Foresters' fifteen men reported missing. The struggle still continued. On 18 May the unfortunate Germans still holding Les Trois Sauvages were bombarded by British 6-inch howitzers, but they brought in retaliatory and counter-battery fire. A British battery was destroyed near Vadancourt château, and some artillerymen killed.

North of Gricourt, progress was better towards Pontruet where the 17th Lancashire Fusiliers discovered bridges across the River Omignon that had been abandoned. The incoming 23rd Bn Manchester Regiment found the village of Pontruet itself deserted, the enemy having withdrawn to a crater at the Sainte-Hélène crossroads.

Instructions now went out to all battalions: patrols must be sent out, to keep in touch with the enemy. One such patrol was sent out by the 20th Lancashire Fusiliers on 30 April to reconnoitre the copse known (after a British officer) as Somerville Wood, near Sainte-Héléne. It proved to be something of a hornets' nest, and the patrol came under strong enemy fire at close range. Both the patrol's officer (Second Lieutenant Gibbons) and his NCO were hit and a third man killed; a later patrol to seek the dead and wounded failed to find the young officer, whose name appears on the Thiepval Memorial.

The German retreat and the Allied pursuit were now almost complete, with the British army holding a front that ran from the French army at Dallon round to the north near Pontruet: the German-occupied city of Saint Quentin was now stoutly protected by the almost impregnable Hindenburg Line stretching round its western side.

From 20 May 1917 the area passed under the command of the French XI Corps, as fresh projects demanded the presence of the British army elsewhere - but they would be back.

The aftermath of heavy British bombardment.

Chapter Six

PRELUDE TO DEFEAT

1917 was a particularly difficult year for all the war leaders. After the set-backs of 1916 (Verdun and the Somme), the Allied chiefs of staff sought new ways of advancing; but in the French army there were stirrings which led to mutinies after the failure of the Chemin des Dames offensive in April - May 1917, and for a period thereafter the French forces were not able to support their British partners extensively. The British commanders, meanwhile, were planning their next offensive in Belgium. The French forces held the line around Saint Quentin from approximately May - December, by which time the addition of the Americans to the Allies was beginning to make a difference to plans on both sides of the Western Front.

In December 1917 the Supreme War Council decided that more of the Allied front line should be held by the British and in January 1918 the Fifth Army, under General Sir Hubert Gough, was therefore moved south to take over from the French army facing the Hindenburg Line.

March 1918, The Fifth Army's battle area.

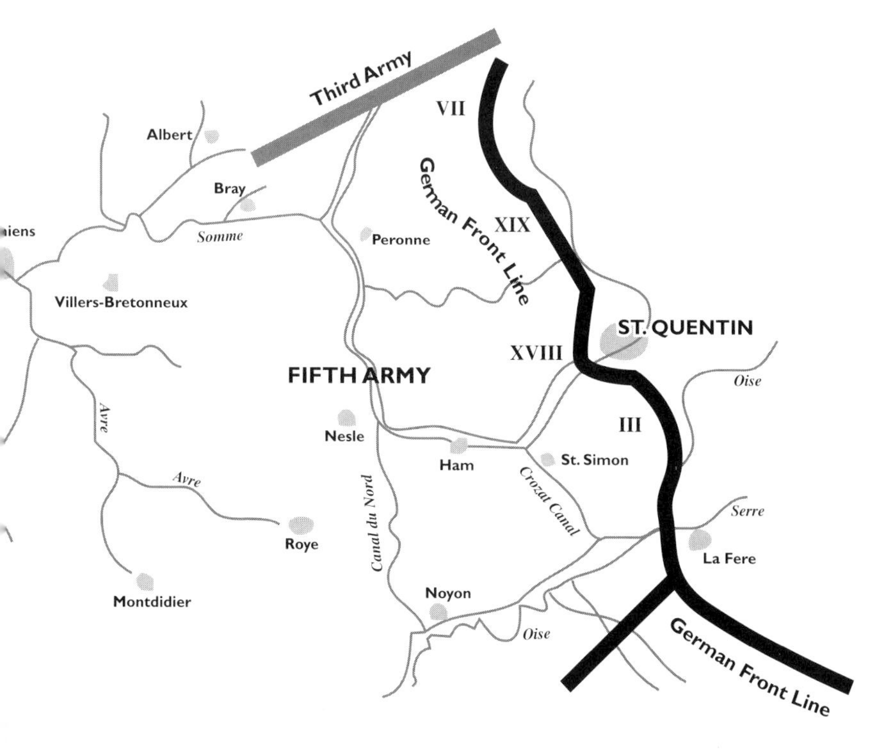

Although there were said to be well over 400,000 men in British regimental depots at home, available for posting overseas, the British Army was notably under strength on the Western Front at this time; and the shortage of men in the Fifth Army was accentuated by its allocation to a front of 42 miles, from Gouzeaucourt in the north to beyond Chauny in the south. Compared with the Third Army's front line, adjacent to the north, which ran for only 26 miles and faced 24 divisions, General Gough and his army was opposed by 43 German divisions. Some nine miles of Gough's very extensive front line were taken up with holding the trenches round the city of Saint Quentin itself.

This sector round Saint Quentin was the responsibility of Lieutenant-General Sir Ivor Maxse, in command of XVIII Corps (including 30th, 36th (Ulster) and 61st Divisions). The inclusion of 30th Division was not Maxse's first choice, but Gough prevailed upon

The Redoubts: British Positions on 20 March 1918.

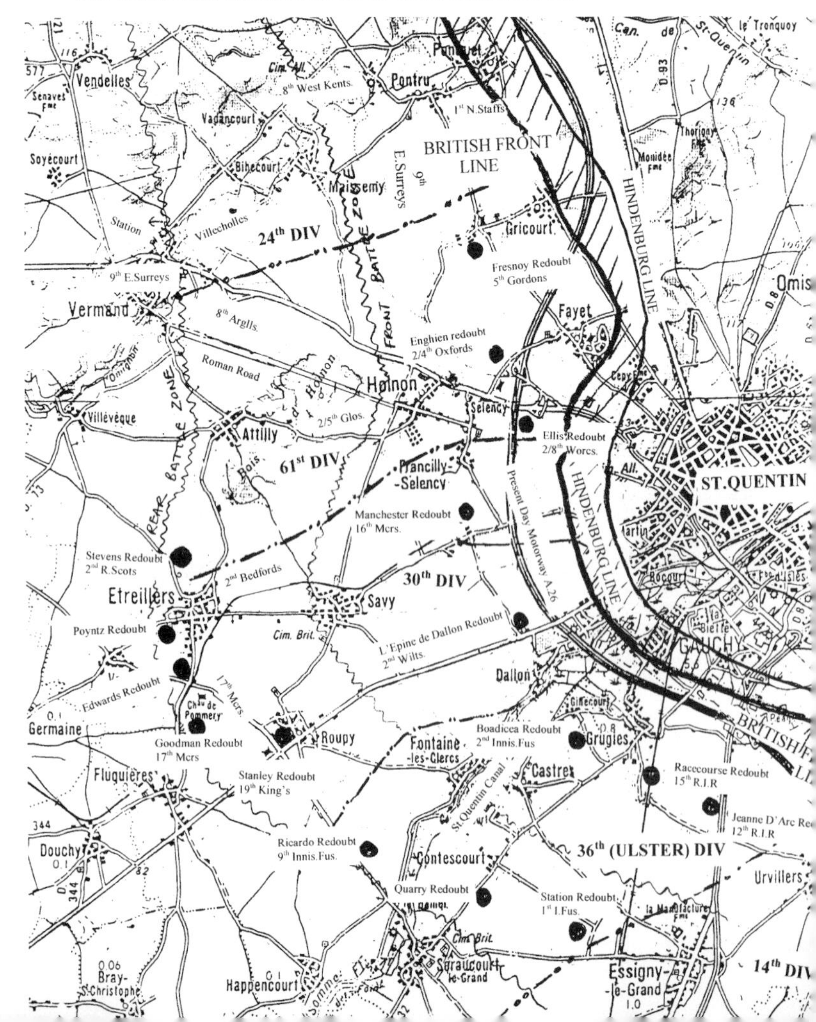

him to take it under his command. In March 1918, three of its nine battalions belonged to the King's Liverpool Regiment (17th, 18th, 19th) and two to the Manchester Regiment (16th, 17th) - battalions which on 1 July 1916 had served with distinction. These former Pals battalions were to continue to fight doggedly, almost to the point of annihilation, through the difficult days to come in the early months of 1918.

The new defence arrangements in front of Saint Quentin included a Forward Zone of trenches and redoubts with outposts set in front and linked by masses of barbed wire. Within this area, counter-attack companies were held in reserve; a Battle Zone extended over some 4000 yards behind it with strongly defended redoubts, counter-attack units and emplacements protected by trenches and barbed wire. The Forward Zone was designed to hold any minor attack and, as far as possible, to break up any larger one; a Rear Zone lay several miles behind the Battle Zone.

The system posed problems for the British artillery. While some field pieces had to be designated for sniping, other sections of guns and limbers had to be allocated to operate in the various zones in a roving capacity. Gun batteries near the front were strongly protected with barbed wire, while artillerymen were instructed that their positions were to be regarded as strong points of obstinate defence. All the behind-the-scenes artillery planning was designed to support the infantry battalions when required.

In the case of the 36th (Ulster) Division, these apparently formidable defences were comparatively lightly held, with one battalion for each 2,000 yards of front. The work of constructing the essential trenches, roads, railways, huts etc., and supporting redoubts, had barely begun; and when labour eventually arrived it had just two weeks to carry out several months'-worth of labour. Later in the retreat, units expecting to occupy deep trenches in the Rear Zone discovered that only the top turves had been removed.

With hindsight it is easy to see that there was no realistic prospect of stemming the German attacks: shortage of manpower, inadequate defence works, new procedures - such factors did not raise confidence.

According to one theory, this was a deliberate strategy on Haig's part, offering a recognisable 'weak point' for any German breakthrough which was preferable to collapse on the Ypres front: better Saint Quentin than an immediate threat to the Channel ports.

In the event, this proved accurate, Ypres held out and the Channel ports did not fall.

The impending enemy offensive in the spring of 1918 was fore-

General von Hutier

shadowed by news from captured German deserters, while the intensity of explosions in response to British shells fired at the enemy lines indicated the quantity of ammunition dumps prepared for the assault. As to the German command facing the British, General Gough benefited from a stroke of good luck: the death of a young German pilot shot down in the British lines led to a letter in a German newspaper expressing the sympathy of General von Hutier to the airman's mother. British Intelligence operating in Switzerland noticed the letter, related the General's name to the pilot's known unit at Saint Quentin - and therefore deduced that von Hutier was now in command there. Von Hutier was known for his skill in penetrating enemy lines and included in his staff a Colonel Bruchmüller, known as 'Durchbruch Müller' ('Breakthrough Müller').

Eight Forward Zone redoubts were strung out round Saint Quentin, like beads on a necklace along the outpost trench lines that faced the city and the Hindenburg Line. Of the three British divisions holding the front line opposite Saint Quentin, the 61st Division to the north of the city held three redoubts, three lay in the zone allocated to the 36th (Ulster) to the south and the 30th Division facing the city between them held two.

Benefiting from a favourable wind on 19-20 March 1918, three 'Special Accessory' companies of the Royal Engineers released hundreds of drums of chlorine gas on German troops holding positions in and around the town. The British artillery added their bombardment.

It was completely unexpected, many of the Germans were asleep and, waking, dashed out to meet the supposed British attack - fully armed but without gas masks. An eye-witness account tells of the men dying in great pain from the gas inhalation.

By 1 a.m. the next day, 21 March, the German troops were ready to go forward from their trenches round Saint Quentin. It was a still night, a ground mist was forming and fog enveloped the area. Colonel Bruchmüller's barrage was set to fall on the British troops; the signal would come at 4.40 a.m., when the German garrison in Saint Quentin fired off a white rocket.

From south of Arras in the north to La Fère in the south, the German spring offensives in 1918, Operations Mars and Michael, were about to begin, with the German artillery wreaking havoc along the front and miles behind it. In a field off the Roman road west of Vermand, at Mons en Chaussée, No. 5 (Naval) squadron were shelled out of their airfield and forced to move to another aerodrome further back. The last message received at the airfield before the telephone cables were destroyed by shells came from the Royal Flying Corps headquarters: the Squadron Commander said it proved that 'the Staff could carry on under any circumstances'. The message gave details for providing vegetables during the current shortage and instructions on constructing frames to propagate vegetable seedlings!

(This contrasted with the Squadron Commander's professional skills: Major S. J. Goble, an Australian air 'ace', achieved an amazing feat just before the German offensive when, flying with another pilot at the controls, he brought down two German fighter aircraft with the rear cockpit machine-gun. He later had a distinguished career in the Royal Australian Air Force.)

The German bombardment, opening early in the morning on 21 March, marked the beginning of a serious defeat for the British army. The four British divisions in the Saint Quentin perimeter (24th, 61st, 30th and 36th), handicapped by fog, faced an immensely powerful attack pushed through with great proficiency and determination; the misty conditions did not concern the attackers, since any loss of direction was impossible in a shoulder-to-shoulder advance in such huge numbers.

For the first time the British army in France was required to sustain a form of defence which involved holding isolated trenches, strong points and redoubts which relied in turn on successful counter-attacks in the nearby battle zone coming to their aid. This was in strong contrast to the accepted pattern of defence; remaining isolated in posts, however well fortified, while German storm-troops passed through in the gaps between the redoubts - leaving the garrisons to be overwhelmed at leisure - was not welcome. Known as 'defence in depth', it proved wasteful in practice, and was not repeated.

Yet the British troops responded as required, and even if their best was not always good enough, at least none of the enemy's frontal attacks succeeded. The German success lay in finding a way round the British flanks, sometimes attacking from the rear, undoubtedly helped by the misty conditions. The British machine guns, blinded by the fog, fired on fixed lines at an unseen target and, as the fog lifted, risked finding themselves running out of ammunition in the presence of advancing German troops.

The result was never seriously in doubt. Short of men, fighting bravely in isolated groups, the garrisons were slowly overwhelmed, with very few men escaping to the rear. The courage of the defence was not unrecognised, however, for the commanders of two of these redoubts (Elstob and De Wind) were subsequently awarded a posthumous Victoria Cross.

It is worth looking at events in these redoubts individually. The 61st Division was no stranger to the Saint Quentin area, having been sent there a year earlier during the German retreat to the Hindenburg Line in March 1917. Indeed, some of its battalions (the 2/8th Worcesters for example) were now operating on the ground over which they had patrolled in May 1917.

At Fresnoy le Petit redoubt on the 61st Division front (the most northern in the Saint Quentin area), the 1/5th Gordon Highlanders

British Artillery, Fresnoy-Le-Petit: Two gunners, on the left, are setting up camouflage. Note the dug-out in the background.

occupied a Forward Zone, with the commanding officer, Lieutenant-Colonel McTaggart, Battalion HQ and one company occupying the Redoubt. The rest of the Battalion was posted in the forward lines towards Gricourt. The Battalion had not expected to serve in this division, for the 61st was a South Midland division formed at Northampton in 1915. Hitherto the 5th Gordons, appropriately for a battalion recruited in north-east Scotland, had felt at home serving with the 51st Highland Division. They regretted the order on 31 January 1918 to join their new Division.

When the German rocket gave the signal at 4.40 a.m. on 21 March, the Gordons almost immediately came under heavy German artillery fire as Colonel Bruchmüller's guns came into action.

Most of the battalion was killed, wounded or at best dazed by the intensity of falling shells in the forward zone and outposts. Handicapped by poor visibility, the Gordons were soon overrun - but in the redoubt, Colonel McTaggart and his force held out until 1.30 p.m. when it was completely surrounded and overwhelmed by the enemy. A mere thirty men managed to get back to Brigade headquarters and Lieutenant-Colonel M. F. McTaggart was taken prisoner. Little remained of the battalion except for those left out of battle in order to form a fresh reconstructing nucleus of officers and men.

One of the Gordon Highlanders' officers, Lieutenant A. E. Ker, was serving on detached duty with the Division's machine gun battalion in the Saint Quentin area. Supported by his sergeant and some wounded men, Ker held up a strong German attack with a Vickers machine gun until his ammunition was exhausted. They then fought off enemy attacks with revolvers alone until they were able to capture a German rifle and some ammunition in a hand-to-hand encounter. They were eventually taken prisoner, despite the effects of mustard gas, having held up some 500 attacking enemy troops; Lieutenant Ker was awarded the Victoria Cross.

On 18 March 1918 the 2/4th Oxford and Buckinghamshire Light Infantry handed over to the 2/5th Gloucestershire Regiment in Holnon. They took up their Forward Zone positions in a sector south of the Gordons, centred on the Enghien Redoubt, just off the Selency to Fayet road near a quarry and a château. Well-sited to meet any attack, its good view to the front covered the British lines at Fayet, Squash Valley and Fig Wood, held by the 2/8th Worcesters (the scene of the 2nd Manchesters' attack in April 1917). It was unfortunate that, as with the other redoubts, when the bombardment and attack opened up in the early hours of 21 March, the foggy conditions obscured the view.

The Enghien Redoubt site. A modern photograph of the site taken from the road from Fayet, a direction taken by the advancing Germans when they captured the position in March 1918. Later, the German army enlarged the fortifications considerably and turned it into a very substantial strong-point. Known to the British as 'The Quadrilateral', in September 1918 it did not capitulate without some days of stubborn fighting.

Before the assault, indeed, Lieutenant-Colonel Wetherall, who knew every corner and turning in his sector, was lost within fifty yards of the redoubt and took 15 minutes to find it again.

As the mist cleared, some fifty German troops came under the Oxfords' rifle and Lewis gun fire on the road from Fayet. Half of them went down. Later in the morning, however, the Oxfords came under repeated attack and were driven back slowly until only No.12 post was intact, about three hundred yards from Holnon. By four o'clock that afternoon the men in the Forward Zone had been overwhelmed, with only the survivors of the redoubt itself, under Second Lieutenant J. C. Cunningham, still in action.

The German mobile mortars and howitzers were out of range of the

The German offensives of 1918

British defences, and sent in their bombs and shells with impunity; by 4.30 p.m. Cunningham was instructed - via the telephone cable to Brigade at Attilly, miraculously still intact - to destroy his telephone equipment and set off back to Brigade HQ with all his men. They were captured on their way back to the rear zone.

Meanwhile, the experience of Lieutenant-Colonel Wetherall was a good example of the confusion and changing fortunes of war. Captured earlier in the action with some of his men, he set off with a soldier, possibly his servant, to Saint Quentin, under German escort, taking the main road down the hill towards the city not far from an adjacent strong point (Ellis Redoubt). When a British 6-inch shell landed close to the group, the German escort rushed for cover and the colonel and his companion seized the opportunity to escape.

All went well until they reached the old British line of April 1917, between Holnon and Round Hill, where a party of Germans was consolidating the line - but eventually they departed and the British pair found a gap through to Attilly and Brigade HQ. Another officer of the Oxfords, Second Lieutenant H. Jones, managed to reach the safety of the British lines with a party of men. Hopelessly lost in the mist as they searched for the Enghien Redoubt, they managed to avoid bumping into a German patrol and began to make their way towards British machine guns - recognisable by their sound. They turned out to be in German hands and, following a route similar that Colonel Wetherall's, Jones and his men finally reached Attilly where Brigade HQ sent them to join the 2/5th Glosters in Holnon.

In front of the Enghien Redoubt, the 2/8th Worcestershire Regiment (part of 182nd Brigade) had taken over a forward position on the lower ground, on 14 March 1918. They also took over a section of the front line straddling the main Saint Quentin road beside a wood, Bois des Roses. One company was put in trenches in Fayet, at Squash Valley and Fig Wood, whilst another was detailed to hold trenches in Fayet village itself. The strongest point in the Worcesters' line was the Ellis Redoubt, about a mile behind the front line near the Bois des Roses. Two battalions of the Royal Warwickshires, the 2/6th and 2/7th, lay in the Battle Zone behind the Worcesters.

The Royal Engineers' heavy discharge of gas on 19/20 March disrupted the life of the 2/8th Worcesters near Fayet, as well as the enemy against whom it was aimed. One of two officers affected, out of nineteen casualties, Second Lieutenant R. H. Hunt, was caught in the British gas cloud as he tried to warn his men to evacuate the line.

St Quentin, The Fayet Road. On 19 March 1918 an officer of the 2/8th Worcesters, confused by a cloud of British gas, took a wrong turning in Fayet village and made his way towards this road into the Saint Quentin suburbs and the German lines. He escaped the next day under cover of darkness.

Confused and half-stifled, he turned the wrong way and set off along the road from Fayet towards Saint Quentin. Escaping injury from a German hand-grenade thrown at him, Hunt reached the suburbs of Saint Quentin, lay low until dark, and made his way successfully back to the British lines.

Corps HQ was still anxious for up-to-date information on the enemy forces opposite. At 10 p.m. on 20 March, therefore, the 2/6th Warwickshires mounted a highly successful raid from the Fayet trenches on the left of the 2/8th Worcesters, sending two of their companies forward from the Battle Zone into the busy trenches. Prisoners were taken from several different German regiments, who stated that their attack would begin the next morning.

British artillery fire was launched on the enemy trenches in and around Saint Quentin, with devastating fire - much of it from large calibre shells - pouring into the city and its outskirts from 2.30 a.m. on 21 March. Ninety minutes later the British ceased firing, the 'Stand To' order was given all along the front, and another forty minutes after that the German attack began.

Events here were similar to those elsewhere in the Forward Zones and redoubts. When the enemy bombardment began at 4.40 a.m. the mist was so thick that it was impossible to undertake effective retaliatory fire. The bombardment ceased at 9.30 a.m. and the German troops came over using their new tactics of by-passing the strong-points and leaving the following troops to deal with the defenders. Fayet village was soon taken, the men of 'D' company waiting in Squash Valley failed to receive orders to mount a counter-attack and the enemy were able to enter Fig Wood, just across the dividing ridge, almost unhindered. The only brief warning, a few moments before he was killed, came from Corporal A.V.Wells, MM, commanding a forward post; although communication between Ellis Redoubt and Brigade had been severed, the cable from Fig Wood to battalion HQ in the redoubt had survived. (Corporal Wells has no known grave. His name appears on panel 41 of the Pozières Memorial.)

With Fig Wood taken, it was not long before 'D' Company, awaiting orders in Squash Valley, came under attack from all sides. Taking advantage of the mist and under the command of Captain Hall, MC, the survivors fixed bayonets and charged down Squash Valley, through the enemy, across the main Saint Quentin road near Bois des Roses, past a lightly-held Worcesters' picquet post and into Ellis Redoubt. The picquet post, occupying a small copse near the redoubt, was soon overwhelmed and one of its officers, Second Lieutenant A.C.H. Adams, killed. (He too is commemorated on the Pozières Memorial.)

The Ellis Redoubt was only partially complete, for work on it had begun only a few weeks earlier. Well-sited, with a clear view of Fayet and the 2/4th Oxfords holding the Enghien Redoubt, on 21 March it unfortunately lacked a clear outlook because of the mist until 11.30 a.m. Its garrison, 'B' Company and Battalion HQ, repelled repeated attacks until the Germans withdrew at 2.0 p.m; almost immediately the defenders suffered a tremendous bombardment which wounded the commanding officer, Major Davies, and caused many other casualties.

By this time, large numbers of German soldiers could be seen pouring through Fayet and Squash Valley, attacking the Oxfords who were holding on in the Enghien Redoubt. By 4.30 p.m. it had fallen, its capture leaving the German storm-troopers free to tackle the next redoubt - the Worcesters, in Ellis Redoubt.

The defenders fought on, almost isolated by now, but by 5.30 p.m. the redoubt was completely overwhelmed, with heavy casualties among the defenders: nearly half were killed. Their ammunition exhausted, the survivors surrendered. The Worcesters' stubborn defence of the redoubt had lasted eight hours, and their resistance had so delayed the enemy attack that the Brigade's battle zone to the rear of the battalion was still intact at the end of the day.

The very few men who escaped joined the 'battle reserve' which, together with the survivors of the other redoubts, made up a 'scratch' battalion and departed to a reserve position.

German Officers in Saint Quentin.

Chapter Seven

THE REDOUBTS CONTINUED

There were doubts in the background over the 30th Division. Although it had served with Third Army during the Arras offensives, the XVIII Corps Commander, General Maxse, would rather have had the 58th Division under his command. (He had been particularly impressed by the fighting capabilities of the 2/8 London Regiment (Post Office Rifles) at Ypres in September 1917. This was a 58th Division unit.) There was a suggestion that the 30th Division was no longer what it had been, and was perhaps in need of further training; but Maxse could not refuse General Gough, the Fifth Army Commander, so he took it on, provided some Divisional instruction, and found that it fought well.

The Division had responsibility for two redoubts, Manchester Hill (Manchester Redoubt), held by the 16th Manchester Regiment, and L'Epine de Dallon Redoubt, garrisoned by the 2nd Wiltshire Regiment.

Manchester Hill, with its adjacent quarry, lay south of Francilly-Selency, close to the 2/8th Worcesters of the 182nd Brigade, 61st

Manchester Redoubt. This modern photograph of the redoubt (now hidden within the trees) was taken from the Royal Field Artillery officers' Forward Observation Post in March 1918 in front of the redoubt. The quarry which accommodated the 16th Manchesters' Headquarters and Medical Post in March 1918 and which was stormed by the 2nd Manchesters in April 1917 lies behind the trees.

Division, who were manning the Ellis Redoubt east of Selency. It was on 2 April 1917 that the 2nd Manchesters captured the quarry and the high ground beside it, which was subsequently named Manchester Hill in honour of the battalion's success. Early in January 1918 a sister battalion, the 16th Manchesters (formerly the 1st Manchester `Pals') of the 30th Division, took over and constructed a strong-point which became known as Manchester Redoubt.

Manchester Hill, set on high ground close to the city and overlooking railways and main roads to the west and south, was an important tactical location. The redoubt, trenches and fortifications provided an excellent view of Saint Quentin and gave the battalion good fields of fire in all directions for its machine-guns, trench mortars and riflemen. It provided the principal point of the defence system in the area. In addition a concrete observation post was built inside the redoubt perimeter, for the use of the Field Artillery Forward Observation Officer, well supplied with telephone cable connections to the rear and elsewhere, including Brigade Headquarters. The corresponding disadvantage of the arrangements was that the 16th Manchesters were responsible for holding a sector over a mile wide and some two miles deep. It was a heavy responsibility - and, of course, as they and others were to find, no amount of defences could overcome the thick mist on 21 March 1918.

The redoubt garrison consisted of D company, with Battalion Headquarters including the medical officer, regimental police and quarters for cooks and signallers in the quarry to the rear. In command was the Battalion commander, Lieutenant-Colonel Wilfrith Elstob, DSO, MC. Others of the Manchesters were distributed in the forward trenches, while C company formed a reserve in the rear beside the Saint Quentin - Vermand railway line, near Savy Wood.

Wilfrith Elstob was a remarkable man. Educated at Christ's Hospital and Manchester University, he had been with the 16th Manchesters from its formation in 1914, when he was commissioned as a Second Lieutenant. He rose to command the battalion and even, on occasion, acted as Brigade Commander. Over nearly four years of active service he had served with the battalion on the Somme, at Festubert, Arras and the Ypres fronts - but it was Manchester Redoubt that proved to be the peak of his military career, where he lost his life in the course of winning a Victoria Cross.

Before his men entered the line in March 1918, Elstob emphasised to them that any failure on their part to stem the German advance would mean the sacrifice of others merely to regain ground lost by the

Manchesters. Pointing to the redoubt's position on the map, he stated: 'Here we fight and here we die'.

One of his listeners was No. 6254 Private Charlie Heaton, newly returned from leave in England. Having also been with the Battalion since its formation in 1914, Charlie was known personally by Colonel Elstob, who had been second in command of his company at the time, while the Company Commander in 1914 was Elstob's good friend Captain J. Hubert Worthington. Heaton was taken out of a rifle company and allocated to the Battalion Medical Officer as orderly. The Regimental Aid Post, in a dug-out in the quarry, was run by the 'Yankee Doctor', Captain Walker.

On 21 March 1918 the German bombardment was later in opening fire on the Manchesters than on the neighbouring redoubts - indeed, when Elstob sent out his last patrol at 5.30 a.m. that morning it returned through the thick fog with nothing to report. An hour later, however, the Manchesters' position was suffering under heavy enemy shelling, with the fog intensified by smoke from the bursting shells. The elaborate system of defence set up by the Battalion so confidently and painstakingly just a few weeks earlier was ineffective.

After another hour, at 7.30 a.m., the Battalion front was still intact, but about an hour later a runner reached the redoubt with news that the forward companies were now surrounded. It seemed likely that they would be forced to capitulate, observation was impossible and the complex defence system devised to protect the Manchesters' forward company and eliminate German attacks was useless in the enveloping fog and smoke. The redoubt defenders stood by grimly, powerless to help.

The outlying companies were eventually overwhelmed by the steady enemy attack, the survivors taken prisoner, and Manchester Redoubt by-passed. The intelligence received by General Gough earlier in the year, that he would be facing the German General Hutier, well-known for his skill at penetrating and infiltrating defence lines and supported by the artillery specialist 'Durchbruch' or 'Breakthrough' Müller, proved correct as the two specialists concentrated their skills on the embattled Manchesters.

By late morning the Forward Observation Officer had returned from Manchester Redoubt and reported that Elstob and the Manchesters were holding out there. By this time, however, the Germans were beginning to advance and when the fog cleared, by 11.30 a.m, orderlies sheltering in the Regimental Aid Post in the quarry were amazed to see long files of German soldiers walking steadily past the redoubt on each side of it, paying little attention to its defenders. The system of mutual defence and the anticipated support of the reserve company, on which so much had depended, had been defeated by the combination of fog and overwhelming enemy numbers.

As the German troops by-passed Manchester Redoubt, infiltrated the British lines by Francilly-Selency and moved on towards Savy village, the redoubt stood isolated and alone, while Lieutenant-Colonel Elstob and his men awaited the inevitable arrival of the German 'follow-up troops' to capture it. Elstob moved his headquarters from the quarry to the redoubt, just ahead of the assault on its outlying posts.

The Field Artillery battery's position near the redoubt was now in danger of being overrun and it was therefore ordered to form a new gun line at Etreillers. The gunners departed for the Battle Zone with their teams of horses drawing the guns and limbers, leaving a section in Holnon Wood to cover the withdrawal.

Once the attack began the fighting was intense, with Elstob leading his men in person against the repeated but vain German attempts to bomb their way into the redoubt. In a change of tactics, a brief but sharp artillery bombardment was followed by a very strong attack which the Manchesters just managed to throw back - but the intensity of the German assault was beginning to tell.

When the Germans began their bombardment and attack on the 16th Manchesters, on 21 March 1918, the Hon. Herbert Asquith (son of the British Prime Minister, 1908-1916) was serving with the Royal Field Artillery battery in the gun line just behind Manchester Hill. He later described the day in detail, and it was now his turn to go forward as an observation officer. With his signaller, he made his way up to Round Hill.

As Asquith reached the top of the hill he could see that Manchester Redoubt was now completely surrounded, with a large number of German soldiers forming up nearby, although the shrapnel from his guns bursting round them forced them to change direction towards the Saint Quentin - Vermand railway line.

By 2 p.m. a message from Elstob to Brigade indicated that most of his men in the redoubt were dead or wounded and that enemy soldiers had penetrated it in places. His men were engaged in hand-to-hand fighting. At 3.30 p.m. he contacted Brigade HQ to say that the end was near, then the telephone line went dead, the cable cut. Challenged by the attackers to surrender, Elstob - by now wounded three times - responded 'never' and fell back, shot through the head.

Captain Worthington tried to find and identify Elstob's body after the war, but without success - enemy officer uniforms were frequently removed from the dead, to provide information or to be used in future espionage attempts. Wilfrith Elstob is commemorated on the panels of the Pozières memorial.

With the Enghien and Ellis Redoubts about to fall, it was inevitable that Manchester Redoubt would go too. Their Commanding Officer dead, overcome by superior forces, threatened by mortars close at hand, out of ammunition, the garrison was forced to surrender.

Shortly before his death, in order to bring an approaching German gun battery to a halt, Colonel Elstob ordered his men to fire directly at the legs of a team of horses bringing up the guns along the Saint Quentin - Savy road; and when the group of English prisoners admitted that they had been responsible for shooting the German battery horses, its commanding officer threatened to have them shot. Fortunately for the group, which included the veteran Private Charlie Heaton and his comrades, there was no machine-gun available to carry out the order. Heaton and the rest of the group were ordered to walk slowly towards Saint Quentin, indicating that they were prisoners of war. Their safe passage into the city and imprisonment was assured when German doctors ordered them each to pick up a wounded German soldier and take him into Saint Quentin for medical attention. The little group of British survivors handed over their burdens and were taken off to a prisoner of war compound. (Although out of danger, the prisoners were hungry and thirsty: despite the redoubt's ample supplies, the company's cooks had been sent away and the assault on Manchester Redoubt had fallen on an extremely hungry garrison.)

There were some who escaped. Private Rudge, Elstob's orderly, managed to evade capture and on his return to Brigade Headquarters reported that the Colonel had been wounded and taken prisoner - so that his family became one of many who for a time harboured false hopes of eventual good news.

Away in the distance behind Manchester Redoubt, one unknown British soldier could be heard firing his Lewis gun as his captured comrades trooped off to Saint Quentin. He did not survive long, and the firing ceased as his post was destroyed by the heavy German mortar fire. It was the end of British opposition in the area.

L'Epine de Dallon Redoubt

This strong point, also one of those of the 30th Division, was formed out of a series of ruined houses to the west of Saint Quentin, near the road from the city to Roupy. The redoubt was occupied by the

2nd Wiltshire Regiment, and became Battalion Headquarters under Lieutenant-Colonel A. V. P. Martin. After a quiet day on 20 March, the Battalion War Diary reported that at about 4.30 a.m. the next day an intense bombardment was launched against the Battalion - mostly high explosive and gas shells. In the early hours of 21 March, 30th Division ordered the Wiltshires to send out a patrol of platoon strength and report back: it set off into the thick mist, and was never seen again.

Here, as with all the redoubts and forward positions in action on 21 March, the heavy mist was a handicap to the defenders. When two divisions of German infantry launched their assault at 10 a.m. they quickly broke through on the Battalion's flanks and at about midday Lieutenant Capp and six men of the Wiltshires reported to the Commanding Officer of the 2nd Green Howards, at Roupy, that the Wiltshires were completely surrounded in the redoubt. He and his half-dozen men were the only ones to escape.

The Wiltshires put up a strong resistance against the surrounding German troops, but were eventually overwhelmed. The redoubt was still holding out at 1.30 p.m., for a carrier pigeon sent by Lieutenant-Colonel Martin, the Commanding Officer, stated that they were still resisting despite being reduced to only fifty men. Soon afterwards it was captured.

For several days the first entry in the 2nd Wiltshires' War Diary read, 'No news from the Battalion'. After the war it was learned that several officers and men had been killed and wounded, but many others were taken prisoner along with Colonel Martin.

The 36th (Ulster) Division and the Redoubts

When Sir Ivor Maxse took over his new command in January 1918 he must have appreciated having the 36th (Ulster) Division in his Corps. Veterans of many battles, they had served with distinction at various times with the Second, Third, Fourth and Fifth Armies. Most recently they had taken part in the Battle of Cambrai in November 1917. They now moved to the outskirts of Saint Quentin and the formidable Hindenburg Line to relieve the French who held that part of the front. Taking over from their French allies was more complicated than a changeover with a British Army unit. Procedures differed, ammunition too, and the language question could be a challenge. The one feature that appears consistently in many British diaries is the warm French welcome to their allies: splendid meals figure prominently in the descriptions, with the number of courses and the quality of food and wine carefully described.

The front that they took over lay to the south-east of Saint Quentin, from just beyond the main road from Saint Quentin to La Fère opposite Sphinx Wood to a point near Gauchy on the southern outskirts of the city itself. The Division's front, facing north-east, was flanked to the right by the 14th Division of III Corps. As with the 30th and 61st Divisions to the west, the 36th Division's defence lines included the usual Forward and Battle Zones and a series of redoubts and strong-points. Also like their neighbours, the heavy mist hampered vision and movement as the German attackers advanced, and here too the British units were to be overwhelmed in the end after stubborn resistance.

When the Ulster Division had completed their take-over from the French troops they found plenty of work to do: there was very little barbed wire in place, and new trenches must be dug. As the work proceeded doubts grew about the defence scheme, particularly relating to the gaps between the redoubts and strong-points; these same misgivings were felt by their comrades in the other divisions - but the division felt reasonably well-prepared by the time the assault came on 21 March.

The Divisional boundary took in the Saint Quentin canal, where the Field Companies of the Royal Engineers had to prepare demolition charges and prepare to blow the bridges along the canal in case of a German breakthrough. The three redoubts constructed in the 36th's Forward Zone were named, from west to east, Boadicea, Racecourse and Jeanne d'Arc Redoubts.

At 4.35 a.m. the whole Division came under heavy bombardment, high explosive and gas shells with trench mortars and every kind of artillery firing on the outlying posts, redoubts and rear areas. As the cable connections were destroyed runners had to do their best to maintain communication, and artillery help for the battered infantry in the forward zones was almost impossible.

The German infantry attack began at 8.30 a.m. Although it had been expected on the front of the division, from the direction of Saint Quentin, the assault was launched from the right (eastern) flank of the division, striking west towards the Saint Quentin canal and beyond.

The village of Grugies lay a little to the north of Racecourse Redoubt, south of Gauchy, where the French had made such great efforts to get into Saint Quentin in April 1917. Under cover of the thick mist and smoke from the guns the German storm-troopers swept up Grugies valley towards the village, while just over a mile away the Wiltshires were fighting determinedly in L'Epine de Dallon Redoubt.

The men in the Ulsters' forward sector did their best but, like their comrades elsewhere, were always heavily outnumbered. In the misty conditions the machine gunners and riflemen were overwhelmed before many of them could fire a shot; assaulted by parties from all sides, the outlying posts were quickly captured, and the Germans were now ready to move on.

The Ulsters' main front line, facing east towards the Saint Quentin - La Fère road, had not been fully breached and it became clear that the Germans at Grugies had penetrated behind the Ulsters' main positions. In particular, the men in two of the Forward Zone redoubts - Racecourse and Jeanne d'Arc - were now very vulnerable

Of the two, Racecourse Redoubt was in the greatest danger. Lying south of Grugies just over 500 yards along the Saint Quentin - Tergnier railway line, it was built on the railway embankment and was held by Battalion Headquarters and a company of the 15th Royal Irish Rifles under the command of Second Lieutenant Edmund de Wind, a former private in the Canadian army. Although it managed to hold out under repeated attack for some seven hours, the garrison was finally overwhelmed, with de Wind killed in action after being wounded twice while repelling attacks.

Like Lieutenant-Colonel Elstob at Manchester Redoubt in the neighbouring sector, Lieutenant de Wind received a posthumous Victoria Cross and, also like Elstob, his body was never found. He too is commemorated on the panels of the Pozières memorial and Mount de Wind in Alberta, Canada, bears his name in honour of his courage.

As the enemy swept forward, some posts in the front-line trenches survived for a while. Three companies of the 12th Royal Irish Rifles held positions astride the main Saint Quentin - La Fère road, some outlying posts on the eastern side of the road near Sphinx Wood were under strong attack, and Captain L. J. Johnston and C Company held a position called Le Pontchu Quarry to the west of the road. One telephone cable survived from the front line to Captain Johnston and his men in the quarry, and so C company was called forward to support, moving to a position known as Foucard Trench on the main road. Here they held out for four hours against all kinds of enemy attack, including flame-throwers.

The fog lifted, and the men were suddenly able to witness some remarkable sights. To the rear, about a mile away, they could see men of their Battalion round the Jeanne d'Arc Redoubt engaged in fierce fighting, completely surrounded. The Jeanne d'Arc Redoubt was garrisoned by B company and Battalion H.Q. of the 12th Royal Irish Rifles; it eventually fell around noon.

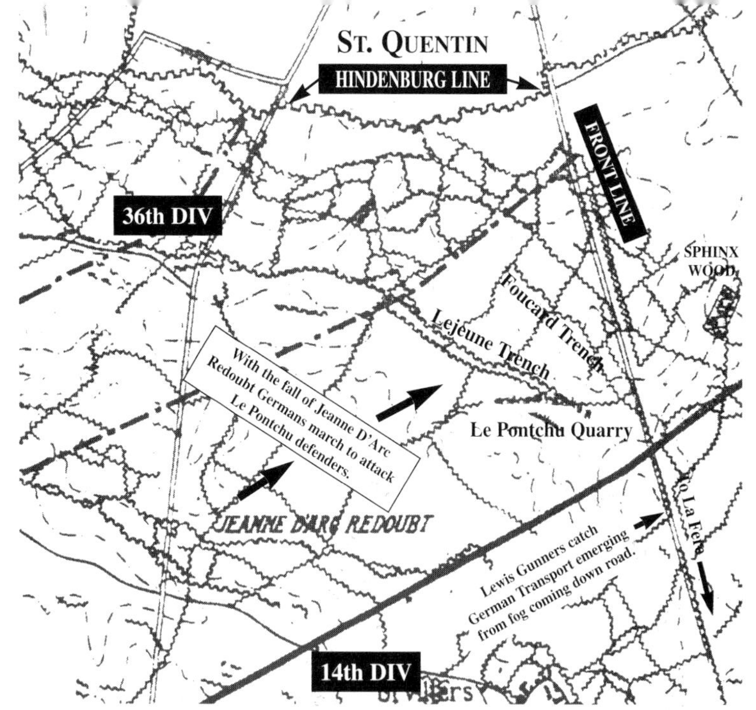

Le Pontchu Quarry: the site of the epic stand by Captain L. J. Johnston and C Coy. 12th Royal Irish Rifles on 21 March 1918.

Across the road to C company's front they could see a squadron of German cavalry in the distance, in the 14th Division's area, and advancing towards them. Closer to hand, a column of German transport was visible to the right of the company, moving slowly down the main road towards La Fère; after a few moments, the company's Lewis guns opened fire at a range of about 400 yards, causing heavy casualties among the surprised transport men.

The company was now under fire from all sides, however, and was soon forced to retreat some 500 yards to a support trench (Lejeune Trench). As they undertook this fiercely contested withdrawal, they admired the offensive courage of the German storm troopers as exemplified by a single German soldier who made a solo charge with fixed bayonet at C company's line.

Reinforcements now arrived from the Forward Headquarters in Le Pontchu Quarry, and Captain Johnston now had some hundred men under his command, ready to face the next attack. It was not long in coming, for by now Jeanne d'Arc Redoubt to the rear of the company had fallen and the way was clear for German 'mopping up' troops to deal with C company's stubborn resistance. Evidently underestimating the task before them, a company of German troops marched out from the captured Jeanne d'Arc Redoubt, in column of fours: as Captain

Johnston was able to record later, when the men of 'C' company opened fire, none of the attackers escaped.

The position was becoming hopeless, however, and the threat of a German tank coming down the road from Saint Quentin while an enemy battalion advanced towards them meant that there was no alternative but to surrender. The survivors were despatched down the Saint Quentin road towards their captivity - but were consoled as they went by the sight of the total destruction wrought by their fire on the German transport column. When the prisoners of war returned after the Armistice, their achievement was acknowledged by seven awards for gallantry.

For some reason Boadicea Redoubt, garrisoned by Battalion HQ and one company of the 2nd Royal Inniskilling Fusiliers, had almost completely escaped the German bombardment. It therefore presented a formidable obstacle to the approaching German infantry, who were reluctant to attack. The Divisional history records a fight against incredible odds, ending at about 5.30 p.m. when the commander decided that further resistance was impossible; it also records that two pigeons found in the redoubt were released by the Germans, and subsequently reached Divisional Headquarters with messages stating that the redoubt was now in German hands.

Historical records of the German Infantry Regiment No. 463 state that after a parley with English-speaking German soldiers, the redoubt's defenders, a wounded lieutenant-colonel and 251 men, surrendered and marched out.

Men in the Forward Zone who could fall back to the Ulsters' Battle Zones were ordered to do so, with one exception at Contescourt, which was then holding up well but was soon to fall. One artillery battery delayed too long in withdrawing its guns when attacked by machine-gun and rifle fire at close quarters - but before they were forced to retire, the gunners managed to immobilise their guns by removing breech blocks and sights.

Beyond the 36th Divisional boundary to the west of the canal, the 30th Division battle zones were still intact, as was that of its neighbours, the 61st Division to the north. To the east, however, the Ulsters' position was 'becoming dangerous', for substantial progress had been made by the enemy thrusting aside the 14th Division's defences on the Ulsters' right flank.

To the east of Saint Quentin, the 14th Division, part of III Corps and next to the Ulsters, had suffered very badly in the German attacks. Conditions in the outlying posts and Forward Zone almost exactly matched those in the zones held by the other divisions holding the front

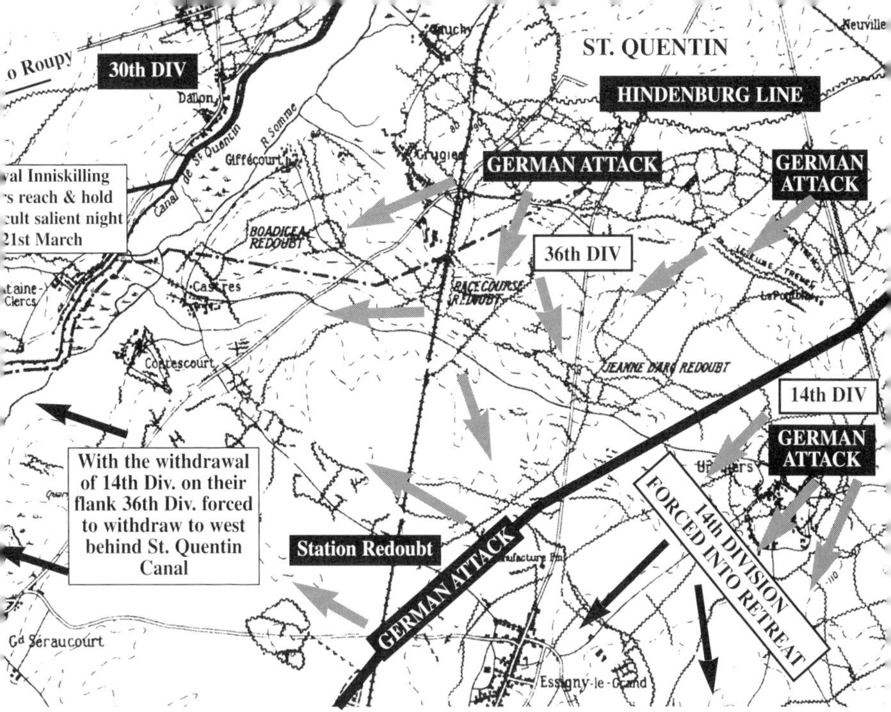

The Retreat of 14 & 36 Divisions, 21 March 1918, from the south-east sector in front of Saint Quentin

line round Saint Quentin; telephone cables were cut, thick mist prevented visual signalling and a tremendous bombardment around 4.30 a.m. was followed by gas shells.

By 10.30 a.m. the enemy were through the 14th Division's Forward Zone and well on their way into the Battle Zone beyond. There were, however, some memorable stands by battalions in these sectors - in particular the 8th Rifle Brigade near Essigny le Grand, knowing the importance of the position, held the German attack for several hours before they were forced to withdraw during the afternoon.

Near the 8th Rifle Brigade around Essigny, two companies of the 11th King's Regiment (Liverpool) (B and C) were in action. This was a Pioneer unit, having been an infantry battalion until 1915; their primary task was to provide skilled labour to other units - one description of them was 'work horses'. They were not expected to act in a fighting capacity, although circumstances sometimes forced them into action, to their delight. Here they were soon involved, and eventually moved near to Benay - after which, nothing more was heard of them. Four of their men, however, captured and despatched unescorted to the enemy lines, managed to escape and rejoin the battalion. Another group broke out, made their way to the British lines and joined a much-depleted artillery battery that was still in action.

With the gunner officer desperately short of men, the Kingsmen were promptly enrolled as temporary gunners.

The Battalion lost a tremendous amount of kit - blankets, stores, cookers, a water cart, all had to be abandoned. The canteen, packed with food, tobacco and provisions of all kinds, had to be left, while a newly-established Church Army rest hut fell into enemy hands.

Some 5000 yards east of Essigny le Grand, the 6th Somerset Light Infantry, holding the forward positions, reported a new kind of gas - mustard gas - which produced a not particularly unpleasant smell but had a soporific effect. At 10.00 a.m. their forward positions were attacked by massed formations of storm troopers, marching shoulder to shoulder and singing as they advanced. Slowly the Somersets were pushed back, although at least one post held out until 6.30 p.m. before it was forced to surrender.

Essigny le Grand and the very large farm complex on its northern edge, known as Manufacture Farm, were garrisoned by the 7th Rifle Brigade. Their stubborn resistance against trench mortar fire, artillery bombardment and flame-thrower attack held off the assaults until mid-afternoon, but finally it was overwhelmed and the British army lost a vital defence point. Its resistance was stoutly supported by two guns of the 36th Machine Gun battalion, which for some time managed to pre-

Manufacture Farm. A modern view of this large farm just outside Essigny-le-Grand. As part of the front line in the 14th Division's battle line on 21 March 1918, its capture by the Germans immediately threatened the garrison in Essigny, leading to flank attacks on the neighbouring 36th (Ulster) Division and a withdrawal to the west.

vent the enemy troops from reaching Essigny railway station, but all resistance seems to have ceased around 3.30 p.m.

This meant that the enemy was able to enter Essigny-le-Grand and move westwards towards Essigny station and Seraucourt-le-Grand. Station Redoubt stood in their way on high ground beside the road just beyond the station, held by the HQ Company of the 1st Royal Irish Fusiliers of the 36th (Ulster) Division - for the enemy troops were now entering another Divisional sector. The German troops came under heavy machine-gun fire but were eventually to overcome it and press on westwards, through Seraucourt-le-Grand and beyond.

As 14th Division's Forward and Battle Zones were gradually overwhelmed, the 36th (Ulsters') flank was being turned. The Ulsters had previously identified the position as 'becoming dangerous', and by mid-afternoon on 21 March their situation confirmed this premonition.

In the Battle Zone, the 7th King's Royal Rifle Corps were completely overwhelmed by much larger numbers; their Commanding

Officer, Lieutenant-Colonel J.G. Birch, was taken prisoner with six of his officers. When the expected enemy frontal attacks failed to materialise, the defending troops were in some cases misled - to the extent that men were sent down into dug-outs for breakfast, leaving the minimum of sentries on look-out. This proved fatal, for with the trenches by-passed by storm-troopers and many men out of the trench, the few sentries on guard were easily overwhelmed by the 'mopping-up' troops following on some time after the initial attacks.

After the war an officer from 14th Division who had been captured in the fighting recounted his experiences. Taking refuge in a shell crater and looking upwards to the rim, he saw several German soldiers levelling their rifles at him, but when he was able to speak to them in German they hesitated and allowed him to climb out of the hole. He was quickly stripped of all valuables and there was a move to take his boots - their own were badly worn. The 14th Division officer pointed out firmly that he was a wounded officer of the British army, and asked to be sent to a dressing-station promptly. This he was allowed to do, on condition that he helped to carry a wounded German soldier to the rear.

During the day's action the Royal Flying Corps was very active in support of the British infantry, harassing the German troops whenever possible. At Urvillers, north-east of Essigny-le-Grand, the 2nd Bavarian Regiment was attacked by R.F.C. bombing aircraft; moving on, the Battalion's Headquarters' staff found some British dug-outs in a sunken road and adopted them as their temporary headquarters. This was an unwise move, for a reconnaissance aircraft from No. 82 Squadron observed them and promptly made a low flying attack with machine-gun fire and bombs. The H.Q. staff was decimated.

Gunners of a Royal Field Artillery battery which had been rushed in the fog managed to remove the breech blocks before taking up a position on the Benay - Hinacourt road, where they delayed the German attacks for several hours with rifles and machine-guns. Finally, cut off and surrounded, the gunners, under the command of Captain Haybittel decided to withdraw; on their way they captured a German machine-gun and a platoon of infantry.

It was clear that the 14th Division was suffering a breakthrough on the Ulsters' flanks. German troops were south-west of the village of Urvillers, flocking westwards, with Manufacture Farm on the Saint Quentin road to the north of Essigny le Grand in enemy hands.

As the Ulsters were slowly forced to fall back, the situation that the 36th Division staff described as 'becoming dangerous' moved through 'dangerous' to become critical. Around 4.0 p.m. the line was stabilised

Tugny-et-Pont, pre-war scene.

in front of three of their Battle Zone redoubts: Ricardo on the left, Quarry in the centre and Station on the right flank, beside the Saint-Quentin - Tergnier railway line.

Later in the day, 21 March, conforming to General Gough's orders, III Corps arranged for the 14th Division to withdraw behind the Crozat canal near Jussy. The move, which meant that the 36th Division also had to swing back west to new positions and form up on the western bank of the Saint Quentin canal, began at 10.30 p.m. and ended almost without enemy interference in the early hours of 22 March.

The 36th Ulsters' withdrawal had inspired some memorable rearguard actions, such as the 1st Royal Inniskilling Fusiliers who

The bridge at Tugny. A modern view. It was here, on 22 March 1918, that Lieutenant C. L. Knox R.E. won his Victoria Cross for blowing up the bridge over the canal whilst operating under enemy fire. It was one of twelve bridges over the Saint Quentin canal which had to be destroyed that day.

fought on until ordered to retire to the Zone's HQ in the Ricardo Redoubt. Enemy troops surrounded the Redoubt and bombers gained a footing inside it; throughout 21 March the defenders continued to fight in its north-west corner to drive them out until, at 6 p.m. that evening, pounded on all sides by mortar fire, the surviving forces within the redoubt, Lieutenant-Colonel J. N. Crawford and a few men, were forced to surrender.

Despite their flank being turned, the Ulster Division had fought hard, but their situation had been hopeless once the 14th Division fell back, and they were eventually forced to make a fighting withdrawal and retire.[3] This had involved crossing the bridges spanning the Saint Quentin canal. Clearly, these bridges could not be left intact once the retreating British had crossed, a responsibility that fell to the Royal Engineers to plan and execute - a difficult operation. Delaying too long would offer the enemy a vital opportunity to rush across before the charges were blown, destroying the bridge too soon would leave comrades on the wrong side, at the mercy of pursuing enemy troops. Most of the engineers' decisions were well judged, although the early destruction of one bridge almost prevented 108th Brigade from getting across.

The steel girder bridge at Tugny was the scene of a near-disaster, for with German troops actually on the bridge the charge failed to fire. At tremendous personal risk, Second Lieutenant C. L. Knox, of the 36th Division's Engineers, climbed under the bridge and lit an instantaneous fuse which he connected to the explosive charge; miraculously, when the charge detonated Lieutenant Knox was not injured and his moment of decision and courage earned him the Victoria Cross.

The 36th (Ulster) Division now lay along the barrier of the Saint Quentin canal with men of the 1st Inniskilling Fusiliers on the Saint Quentin perimeter holding out near Fontaine les Clercs; but during the morning of 22nd March orders arrived for the Division to leave the area, withdraw to the south and take up positions on the Somme Canal between Sommette-Eaucourt and Jussy. The 36th (Ulster) Divisional history records with pride the exploits of their men in this battle, but also recognises the great skill of the well-trained German attackers. In a reference to the American War of Independence, it describes it as 'the greatest defeat suffered by British arms since York Town'.

3. One report of the day records that the Commander of the 14th Division was 'sent home' on 22 March 1918, 'not in a fit state to handle the situation'.

Chapter Eight

THE ALLIED WITHDRAWAL CONTINUES

To the west and north-west of Saint Quentin, 21 March 1918 was also a day of bitter defeat for the men of the 24th Division. The British Army passed through some of the villages here in 1914 during the retreat from Mons - and now their successors were about to retreat again. To the north, the Saint Quentin front line perimeter, which formed an extended semi-circle of trenches round the outskirts of the city, ended here to the north of Pontru, some six miles north of the city.

That morning (21 March), Vermand, and the villages of Pontru, Vadancourt, Maissemy, Bihecourt and Villecholles lay just inside the area occupied by the 24th Division (part of XIX Corps), next to the northern boundary of the 61st Division. Any action involving these six places would affect the defence of the British front line round Saint Quentin.

In the event, the setbacks suffered by garrisons holding the British front line in XIX Corps were almost identical to those of their comrades in other divisions to their right. Struck by a massive bombardment which cut the telephone lines, and handicapped by the thick mist, the men in the front line trenches were rapidly overwhelmed by superior numbers. Here and there sporadic fighting continued where some units managed to hold out.

Early in the morning of 21 March the position of 24th Division units along this line of villages was as follows: 1st North Staffordshire

Vermand village in 1914. British troops retreated through the village in 1914, returned in 1917, and were forced to retreat through it again in March 1918. By 12 September the 1st South Wales Borderers, in pursuit of the retreating enemy, had passed through the village and established a trench line just outside on the road to nearby Villecholles.

A ruin in Vermand. In February 1917, in preparation for their withdrawal to the Hindenburg Line, the German army evacuated all the inhabitants of the villages around Saint Quentin, and destroyed their houses. This is a photograph of 'the only remaining house in Vermand after the German occupation'.

Regiment, in the front line north of Gricourt; 8th Royal West Kent Regiment on their left flank near Pontru; B company of the 9th East Surrey Regiment, consisting of five officers and 120 Other Ranks under Second Lieutenant A. V. Pratt, lay to the rear of the North Staffs, in a reserve trench east of Maissemy. The East Surreys' other companies - A, C and D - held Vermand. Together, the three battalions formed the 72nd Brigade.

Arriving in the front line three days beforehand, the 1st North Staffs were astonished to realise that they were to occupy trenches along a front of 2000 yards, from just north of Gricourt to an area in front of Pontruet. The dug-outs were poor and the barbed wire defences inadequate, for most of the work in this sector had been concentrated on fortifying a strong-point, the Essling Redoubt, on high ground behind them half-way along the Pontru - Fresnoy road.

By 21 March, most of the battalion were holding the forward trenches, although one company was later sent to garrison the Essling Redoubt to the rear. The North Staffs Battalion HQ set up a defensive position on a sharp slope on the road out of Maissemy towards Saint Quentin, constructing dug-outs in the steep banks along the road and also a concrete observation post.

Arrangements for the day included plans for the Divisional Artillery to fire regular bursts of harassing fire across No Man's Land at various specified intervals; it was at 4.30 a.m., during one of these bursts, that the heavy German bombardment began. With none of the telephone cables below ground, communication with any of the North Staffs' company positions was almost immediately impossible except by runner - but eventually a daring motor-cycle despatch rider reached the North Staffs' Battalion HQ near Maissemy from Brigade HQ, ordering the manning of all stations in the Battle Zone. No prompting was needed.

The German bombardment ceased in due course, but, as elsewhere, the thick fog hid any enemy approach. This took the form along the

Vermand-Marteville Railway station. The station in 1999 (top) and in 1918 after being badly damaged during the war (right). Part of the original Saint Quentin-Savy-Vermand-Bihecourt line, the permanent way has long since been removed and the station is now used as a road maintenance depot.

North Staffs' front line trenches of up to ten waves of attacking storm troopers. As they charged, the leaders of each wave fired automatic weapons; in the case of any resistance they passed round the defence post, leaving their followers to eliminate it. Under such large numbers the forward posts were soon overwhelmed, despite fighting for as long as possible; after very fierce fighting the companies manning the forward trenches were almost wiped out and the survivors taken prisoner. The regiment was only able to establish the facts after the end of the war.

With the North Staffs in the forward area now out of the fight, the German forces swept on. By 11 a.m. they had reached the reserve trenches held by B company of the 9th East Surreys, just north-east of Maissemy. The defenders held off the attack for about an hour but just after noon, reduced to fifty men and with ammunition running short, their trench was rushed and the survivors captured; some thirty NCOs and men managed to escape and rejoined the Battalion, by now at Villecholles outside Vermand.

The adjacent 61st Division was under instructions to provide a

21-22 March 1918,the sector north of Saint Quentin. The roads and villages marked were familiar to the British Army retreating in 1914 from Le Cateau to Vermand via Bellenglise. The map also covers the area of fighting during the German retreat to the Hindenburg Line in 1917 and again in September 1918 during the 'Advance to Victory'. (Note that the 2/5th Glosters fought in the area both in 1917 and 1918.)

Battalion to cover a difficult part of the front south of Maissemy, and a young Highlander officer reached the North Staffs' battalion HQ outside Maissemy to report that the 1/8th Argyll and Sutherland Highlanders were now in position to the south of them, a very welcome reinforcement even though his commanding officer, Lieutenant-Colonel Macalpine-Downie had been killed before the Argylls had even left their billets. (In fact he had been badly wounded there, and died later in the day).

The Argylls' defensive position lay south-east of Villecholles, fac-

Pontru Château, 1914. In March 1918 the ruins of this once very elegant château formed part of the left flank of the 1st North Staffs' front line. Despite their efforts, and those of the 8th West Kents, the position was in enemy hands by early morning of 21 March.

ing north - a flank that the Germans were desperate to break through, for it would ease their currently very crowded situation. In addition, a breakthrough here would open the way to Holnon Wood and a rear attack on the British battalions in the 61st Division's Battle Zones, particularly the 2/5th Glosters along the Saint Quentin - Vermand road. An attempted counter-attack launched by the 2/4th Royal Berkshire Regiment at 4.30 p.m. was defeated, when Lieutenant-Colonel J. H. Dimmer (who had won the Victoria Cross in the Ypres salient in November 1914) decided that, unusually for one of his rank, he would lead a column of reinforcements at the head of his men. To give extra weight to this morale-building gesture, he set out on horseback, accompanied by a groom - but this offered a perfect target to the waiting troops, and Dimmer was shot dead. (His grave is in Vadancourt military cemetery.)

Later in the day, another German attack on the Argylls failed to get through - and the 61st Division's flanks were still intact at the end of 21 March, against all the odds. It was during this battle that Second Lieutenant John Buchan of the Argylls gained the posthumous award of the Victoria Cross.

With the North Staffs' forward posts overrun, Essling Redoubt was soon under attack from all sides, with the sounds of battle easily audible at their Battalion HQ near Maissemy. By noon the garrison in the redoubt had been virtually destroyed. (One popular officer, Captain Philip Harris, had chosen to live in the redoubt when he was posted to 72 Brigade HQ to recuperate after fierce fighting in the Ypres salient in June 1917. When the attack began, as his batman reported after the war, Captain Harris left the redoubt with revolver in hand, only to be severely wounded by an enemy hand grenade. He died a few moments later and is commemorated on the Pozières memorial.)

The North Staffs' Battalion HQ near Maissemy was next to come under attack. Much of its garrison duties were undertaken by administrative rather than combatant staff - cooks, signallers, storemen, police, officers' servants, etc. On this occasion all were required to fight, and rose to the occasion: the Regimental Sergeant Major, for example, John Brough DCM, seized a rifle, declaring that as a young soldier in 1901 he had been a first-class marksman and would now show the enemy what a British Army marksman could achieve. (This he did, with great effect, but was hit and killed.) By 1 p.m. on 21 March the survivors of the Battalion HQ party were forced to withdraw and were then attached to the 9th East Surrey Regiment - which, by this time, had moved up from Vermand to a ridge near Maissemy.

Vadancourt Château, before the war and eighty years later. The modern view is taken from the remains of one of the trenches dug by the 8th West Kents in March 1918 when they made the grounds and the ruins of the château part of the Fifth Army's Rear Zone. The River Omignon, the ornamental lake and marshy terrain made a good tactical defensive position.

In October 1918 a member of the North Staffs battalion visited the position where the Battalion HQ party had been holding out; the dugouts and concrete observation point had long been destroyed, but he discovered a German memorial near-by which commemorated the deaths of some twenty German soldiers, killed here on 21 March in action against the Staffordshire Battalion HQ. John Brough, the RSM, and his `specialists' had clearly given a good account of themselves.

The day had cost the battalion dear: the Casualty Return for March reported some 652 officers and men as casualties, of whom 214 were killed or wounded. Only 23 came through unscathed.

While B company of the 9th East Surreys was supporting the 1st North Staffs in the early hours of 21 March, the remainder of the Surrey battalion awaited orders in Vermand. After so many false alarms in the past, there were no attempts to move to a defensive position - indeed, when the German barrage fell on the Battalion most men were asleep in their bell-tents.

Clearly the German artillery had found a good target, for this early bombardment wrought great losses on the battalion transport. Horses were killed and wounded, the Transport Officer was wounded while trying to move his transport to safety and several of the signallers were wounded when a shell hit their hut.

At around 10 a.m. orders came through for the East Surreys' three companies to move forward to Villecholles, a village on the bank of the River Omignon near the spot where the river widens into a lake and marsh. As the Commanding Officer, Lieutenant-Colonel Le Fleming, went ahead with a runner to reconnoitre the ground, Major Clark, Second in Command, led the battalion to its new positions as rapidly as possible. As they made their way along the Vermand - Villecholles - Maissemy road, Clark and his men met gunners from a battery that had been attacked and overwhelmed; before leaving they had managed to immobilise their guns by removing the breech blocks, which they were now carrying to the rear. When they reported to Major Clark that the enemy was not far behind them on the road, Clark deployed A company on both sides of the road to meet the advance.

As soon as the East Surreys reached Villecholles, Colonel Le Fleming ordered the Battalion to the high ground east of the village and set off with Major Clark for further reconnaissance. Making their way along a ridge, they came under German machine-gun fire and the colonel was killed instantly. (Colonel Le Fleming's body was recovered but after the war his grave could not be found. He too is commemorated on the Pozières memorial.)

With the enemy making no attempt to move forward, Major Clark crawled back to the crest of the ridge where he met C company trying to advance. Stopped by the heavy machine-gun fire, they withdrew into better cover. At this stage Lieutenant-Colonel Anderson and the 11th Hussars arrived and he took command of the East Surreys.

High Street, Maissemy. Taken just before the outbreak of war in 1914, the photograph shows the village main street looking towards Saint Quentin. At the end of the street, now the D 735 road, the right hand fork led via a sunken road to Holnon and thence to Saint Quentin. In March 1918 the 1st North Staffs established their HQ in this sunken road; the post was overwhelmed by 1 p.m. on 21 March, but not before RSM John Brough, DCM, and his men had taken a heavy toll of the attacking Germans.

Early next day, 22 March, the Surreys and the Hussars came under heavy shell-fire for half an hour, and at 10.30 a.m. defeated a strong attack with accurate rifle and Lewis gun fire. Another attack an hour later was defeated similarly, with heavy German casualties, and a third onslaught just after noon drove in part of the English flank before it was restored with the help (as in the case of the North Staffs) of the East Surreys' headquarters staff.

During these actions on 21 March, the remaining battalion in 72 Brigade, the 8th Battalion The Queen's Own Royal West Kent Regiment, was also heavily engaged in the same area along the River Omignon. Battalion Headquarters were on a ridge running through the grounds of Vadancourt Château, once a magnificent mansion but now a ruin. The area, a well-sited redoubt with a double line of trenches in front, had an excellent field of fire, its tactical position further improved by the defensive value of the marshy ground along the river. A road ran south from this commanding position to the Battalion's right flank at Maissemy, near the position of the North Staffs' Battalion HQ. To the north the battalion had the Bellenglise - Vadancourt road on its left flank and a huge mound about 50 feet high (`The Tumulus') a few hundred yards beyond it. The mound near the out-post line also provided an excellent signalling position; beyond it to the north, the 3rd Rifle Brigade held the front line.

When the bombardment began falling on the West Kents' positions at 4.30 a.m. on 21 March, Vadancourt Château was heavily assaulted by gas shells. The attacking gunnery was outstanding, the targets picked out and destroyed having been located earlier by sound ranging and map reference. (Sound ranging measured time differences in hearing gun reports, and depended heavily on wind direction. It was particularly difficult for the British to gain accurate readings in the west wind which was the prevailing direction for them on the Western Front.)

Most of the supporting British artillery batteries came under very heavy fire from the onset of the barrage, and were quickly put out of action - in one case, two 4.5 inch howitzers were destroyed after firing only a few rounds.

By 10.30 a.m. scouts of the West Kents reported that the 1st North Staffs' lines had been broken and that enemy troops were advancing along the road from Maissemy to Vadancourt. The essential task of destroying the bridge over the Omignon immediately was achieved by Lieutenant Christison, of the Royal Engineers' 103rd Field Company. This made the West Kents secure from frontal attack, but they still suf-

Cooker Quarry and Watling Street: Now surrounded by bushes, the quarry on the left was the scene of heavy fighting on 21 March 1918, involving the 3rd Rifle Brigade. By 7.15 p.m. the garrison had been driven out by the advancing Germans and forced to retreat to Vadancourt (behind the camera position). The road seen here, known to the British troops as Watling Street, leads to Bellenglise beyond the crest.

fered from machine gun fire on their flanks.

While all this was going on, the infantry received considerable help from No. 35 Squadron of the Royal Flying Corps. Its aircrews repeatedly attacked the German troops and their transport near Maissemy, dropping 25lb bombs and firing steadily at the advancing enemy. The crews were also occasionally able to spot targets of enemy soldiers or cavalry and, calling up artillery batteries which were still in action, were able to bring down heavy shell-fire on them. One attack by 1,500 German troops was heavily defeated in this way.

On the West Kents' left flank, however, the Germans advanced rapidly down the road from Bellenglise to Vadancourt until they were stopped by some extremely accurate shooting from Cooker Quarry along the road, held by the 3rd Rifle Brigade. One company of the West Kents in the area was gradually surrounded and eventually ran out of ammunition; the survivors fixed bayonets and charged the German

The Tumulus: in March 1918 this large mound, some 50 feet high, was part of the 8th West Kents' outpost line. Forming a good look-out position from the British trenches, from time to time it attracted enemy fire, the German artillery using it as a registration point for their guns.

Marshal Ferdinand Foch. Prompted by the success of the German offensive in March 1918 and after a conference in Doullens on 26 March at which President Poincaré and M. Clémenceau were present, amongst others, the French general was appointed as Supreme Allied Commander. When given the appointment he responded: 'You give me a lost battle and tell me to win it'.

lines in their attempt to reach the Battalion's main positions - a bold but sadly unsuccessful venture which ended with their capture.

The confidence of the German storm troopers in their advance turned out to be justified: with most of the British field batteries eliminated early in the day, the attackers suffered little return fire. From The Tumulus British observers saw German flag signals, while in the distance enemy reinforcements could be seen moving up in all directions to support the next attacks.

With the bridge blown at Vadancourt the German troops could not approach and take the village from the swamp and the river - the better alternative seemed to be to continue along the Bellenglise - Vadancourt road to take Cooker Quarry and proceed from there. This move was easily fought off by the West Kents, who were adequately armed with Vickers and Lewis machine guns and had every confidence that they could hold on.

Enemy progress westwards through the 1st North Staffs' lines, however, threatened their flank and made it clear that the West Kents would soon have to fall back. As the Germans gained ground steadily to their rear, they successfully fought off several frontal attacks, but with the clearer weather they came under low-level attack from German aircraft. Until 7.30 p.m. the West Kents held on well, still able to use their plentiful ammunition for sustained fire on every attack. Unfortunately, with the 3rd Rifle Brigade unable to hold Cooker Quarry the West Kents no longer had protection on their flanks; at about 8.30 p.m. the battalion made a fighting withdrawal westwards, under cover of darkness, to Bihecourt beyond Vadancourt.

Chapter Nine

THE 30th & 61st DIVISIONS IN ACTION

All round Saint Quentin the British army lines encircling the city had been pushed back considerably by the end of 21 March 1918. The 14th Division was in retreat, by now well away from the city, as was the 36th (Ulster) Division, apart from one Battalion at Fontaine les Clercs, soon to retire.

Very early next day, 22 March, at a 72 Brigade conference in one of the cellars in Vermand, it was agreed that the enemy had achieved very little success on the 72 Brigade front but that the numerical strength of the East Surreys and West Kents was now very low. During 21 March the brigade had lost Lieutenant-Colonel Le Fleming, of the 9th East Surreys, killed in action, and Lieutenant-Colonel Pope of the 1st North Staffs, very severely wounded.

That a good fighting spirit still survived in the brigade, however, was realised by the German troops when they stormed the British front line at Bihecourt early on 22 March; although at one stage they almost reached the muzzles of the British guns, the strong barbed wire entanglements that they encountered led to very heavy German casualties.

The remnants of the Brigade continued to hold their own against continually renewed attacks, but German troops broke through elsewhere; later in the day it became clear that the fighting had reached Bernes, a village some five miles north-west of Bihecourt and well behind the British front. Given the immediate order to retire through Vermand and along the Roman road to the west, the West Kents managed to reach Vermand with the minimum of casualties - something of a miracle, since the withdrawal was made under heavy shell fire along a single road between fields covered in barbed-wire entanglements.

'We were peppered with machine-guns along the road, but we got through!' This reflects the West Kents' actions, and also the conduct of the 9th East Surreys through these two terrible days. Despite their confidence in their own abilities and the courage of defending troops elsewhere along the line, it was impossible to stem the enemy onslaught. As defences broke and left openings for potential flank attacks, the West Kents and East Surreys were forced into a fighting withdrawal - yet holding the ridge north of the River Omignon had made a substantial tactical contribution to the day. In his first despatch on the battle, General Gough made particular mention of these two battalions of the 24th Division.

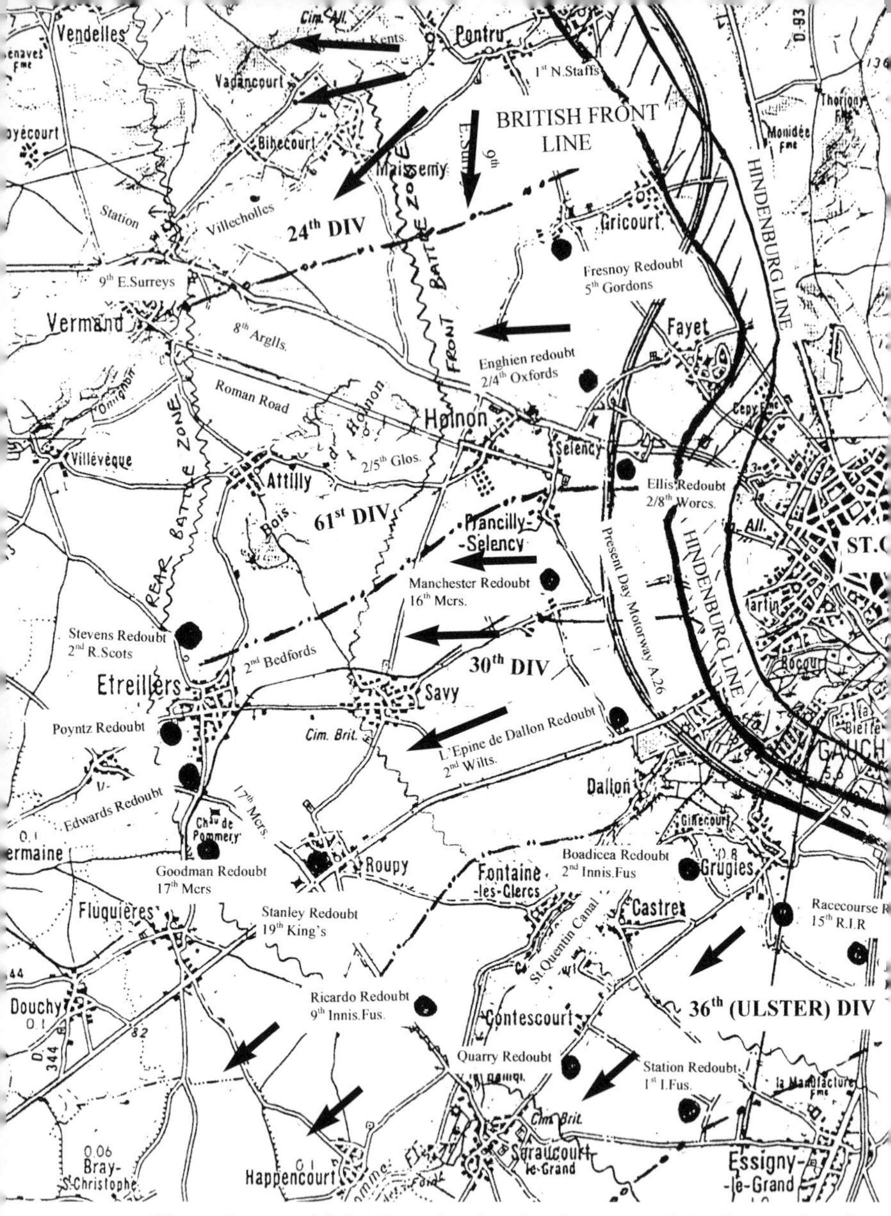

The perimeter of Saint Quentin, showing the extent of the German breakthrough by the early hours of 22 March 1918. The British front line has been broken and all the Forward Zone redoubts have fallen. Most of 24 Division's area has been overrun. 14th Division has been forced into retreat and, as a consequence, the 36th (Ulster) Division's flank has been turned, forcing them to withdraw as well. This left the 1st Royal Inniskilling Fusiliers in a difficult salient at Fontaine-les-Clercs. The line of the Front Battle Zones of the weakened 61st and 30th Divisions, however, is almost intact. The British Army's semi-circle of troops round Saint Quentin has been thrown back and the enemy are about to resume their advance.

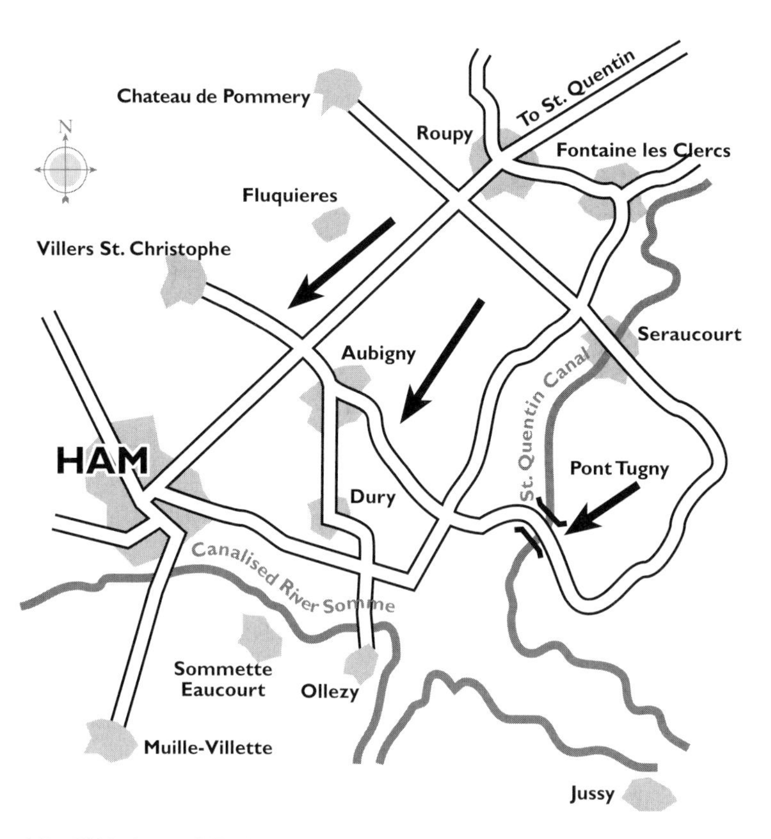

The Fifth Army falls back - the general direction of the British retreat from the Saint Quentin area on 22 March 1918. Note the position of Pont Tugny where Second Lieutenant Knox won his Victoria Cross by blowing up the bridge over the Saint Quentin canal.

The 24th Division in the Vermand area, represented by the East Surreys and West Kents, would soon break off and march westwards. Although two divisions were still operating in the Battle Zone round Saint Quentin - the 30th and the 61st - they too would soon be compelled to withdraw.

The very fierce fighting in the area held by the 30th Division, late on 21 March 1918, involved repeated attacks that were repulsed with the advancing Germans suffering heavy casualties. (See p.89) Savy and Savy Wood had been captured by the enemy. The action was not entirely one-sided, however, for the German troops taking cover in the quarry to the north of Roupy had suffered tremendous damage: later it was established that one British Vickers machine-gunner had fired some twelve thousand rounds of ammunition, while two others had been responsible for firing 35,000 rounds. Roupy Quarry seems to

April 1918: German Officers and a British dugout near Saint Quentin. Note the section of railway track stuck vertically into the ground as support for camouflage material to hide the dugout entrance.

have been a potential death-trap, for it was here that in April 1917 the 16th Highland Light Infantry had lost a number of men under German artillery fire. (See page 61.)

Roupy village itself was still - barely - in British hands and the German attacks, involving heavy artillery fire, tanks and low-flying aircraft, had made no real impression on the Battle Zone near the village. Outside the immediate village area, however, enemy troops were established along the edge of the British trenches and keeps facing towards Saint Quentin, held by the 2nd Yorkshire Regiment (Green Howards) and the 19th King's Regiment (Liverpool). Similarly, German troops now occupied a line of trenches opposite the 1st Royal Inniskilling Fusiliers of the 36th (Ulster) Division in their difficult salient at Fontaine-les-Clercs, to the right of these two Battalions. To the left of the Green Howards and the 19th Kings, the 17th Manchesters stood firm near the Château de Pommery, as did the 2nd Bedfordshire Regiment on the Manchesters' left flank, not far from Savy railway station.

As on the previous day, 22 March opened with heavy morning mist. At around 7 a.m. the Green Howards at Roupy came under strong enemy attack, their left flank was soon penetrated, and they came under machine gun fire from north-west of the village. The attack continued throughout the morning; by 3 p.m. their commanding officer,

Lieutenant-Colonel Edwards, was wounded and on their right flank the 1st Royal Inniskilling Fusiliers had been withdrawn from Fontaine-les-Clercs, leaving the Green Howards in a virtually untenable position.

The first position to which they withdrew, south-west towards Fluquières, turned out to be unsuitable - the lack of labour allocated to the Fifth Army earlier in the year meant that the trenches were only three feet deep, and the Green Howards therefore moved on quickly further to the rear to take up a defence position in Fluquières itself.

Their stay there was brief, for they were still under fire. By about 6.30 p.m. they moved on again, this time taking up new positions on a ridge between Fluquières and Aubigny-aux-Kaisnes. Here the battalion began a reorganization.

Pre-war Roupy. On 28 August 1914, Major Bridges and men of the 1st Royal Warwicks and 2nd Dublin Fusiliers passed through this village during the retreat from Mons. On 22 March 1918 the village, by now in ruins, was the scene of the stand by the 19th King's Liverpools and 2nd Green Howards. The Stanley Redoubt, named after Brigadier-General Stanley, was located at a crossroads near the church.

These attempts to reorganise were interrupted almost immediately by another enemy attack. By 6.45 p.m. a motor-cycle despatch rider brought orders for them to withdraw immediately to Ham; as they reached the town they were instructed to march straight through, taking the Noyon road to Muille-Villette - a well-planned exercise during the exhausting fighting retreat, for travelling field kitchens awaited them with meals ready prepared.[4]

The powerful German pursuit continued and Ham, with its canal crossings, rail junction and important sidings was soon under threat. Just before dawn the next day, 23 March, Brigadier-General Stanley and his Headquarters (89 Brigade) moved out of the town, leaving a party of volunteers 'detailed' to delay the German advance by street fighting. The group included 25 musicians from the Brigade band. Amidst the haste of the departure from this important centre, enormous quantities of military equipment and supplies had to be left behind -

4. By the time that the German offensive began to weaken two weeks later, the Green Howards had been reduced from 623 officers and men to a mere five officers and two hundred Other Ranks. These survivors were now needed elsewhere, and on 5 April 1918 they were despatched to the canal bank north of Ypres in General Horne's First Army.

Roupy village cemetery, modern view. During their offensive in March 1918 German machine gunners fired down from the cemetery walls into trenches in the adjacent fields held by the 19th King's Liverpools.

including some railway engines standing in the sidings with steam up and ready to go, although without crews. A passing soldier emptied his rifle into the boilers, giving each one in turn several rounds of ball ammunition, thus ensuring that the German engineers would not be able to make use of them for some time.

To the left of the Green Howards on 22 March, the 19th Bn. The King's Regiment (Liverpool) was already in action at 1.15 a.m. Part of Roupy village had fallen into German hands and the 19th King's were allocated to recover the lost trenches. On the narrow road from Roupy to Savy the village cemetery lies beside a right-angle bend; it was here that the 19th Kings went into action but although the regimental history records that the trenches were recaptured and that the whole event was 'a very gallant affair', unfortunately all records were lost in the following days of fighting and no exact details survived.

Shortly afterwards the Battalion held another trench line, running past the village cemetery with its Battalion headquarters to the rear in the Stanley Redoubt at Roupy crossroads (named after the Brigade Commander, Brigadier-General F. C. Stanley). At 7 a.m. on 22 March the German offensive was resumed, with further attacks continuing throughout the morning and early afternoon. When at one stage the German machine gunners were firing from the cemetery walls at the Kingsmen holding the trenches in the adjacent field, it was clear that it was only a matter of time before the defenders were overwhelmed. With the Green Howards hard-pressed on their right, and the imminent withdrawal of the 1st Inniskillings at Fontaine-les-Clercs, the situation was deteriorating for both Battalions and late in the afternoon of 22 March the inevitable German break-through happened. The survivors regrouped in Stanley Redoubt, but here too the defenders were over-

The main street in Etreillers, before the war. In March 1918 the village lay in the British Battle Zone and it was near here that the 2nd Bedfords came into action on 22 March during the German offensive.

whelmed: with the commanding officer wounded and no hope of relief, the remnants of the 19th King's surrendered.

The remaining very few men of the Battalion fell back to Ham which they reached in the early hours of 23 March. They took up a position north of the town.

Back in February 1917, as part of the wide-spread destruction that was part of their construction of the Hindenburg Line, the Germans had dynamited the elegant Château de Pommery, and six weeks later the 2nd Manchesters had assembled there before their successful attack on Francilly-Selency. These ruins were now brought into use as a redoubt named after Brigadier-General G. D. Goodman and on 22 March the 17th Manchesters, sister battalion of the 2nd Manchesters, now serving in Goodman's brigade, held the line in this area. The trenches on their right flankwere occupied by the 19th King's Regiment (Liverpool), while the 2nd Bedford Regiment was in trenches near Savy railway station on their left.

With the Germans fully occupied in their assault on their neighbours the 19th Kings and 2nd Green Howards, the 17th Manchesters did not come under attack until the early afternoon of 22 March. They were soon subjected to a very heavy bombardment and after severe fighting the surrounding trenches and strong-points were captured. A Company and Battalion Headquarters in the Goodman Redoubt complex now came under siege and as the German troops steadily gained a footing it was eventually evacuated; the survivors withdrew to the rear, with just over 100 men answering the roll-call when they finally assembled at Muille Villette, south of Ham.

The experiences of the 2nd Bedfords were very similar to those of their comrades in the 30th Division, currently holding the divisional front to their right and south. Battalion defence was based on trenches near Poyntz Redoubt, named after the battalion commander, Lieutenant-Colonel H. S. Poyntz, in temporary command of 90 Brigade. Like their neighbours the 17th Manchesters, after severe fighting in the early afternoon of 22 March the Bedfords were forced to withdraw. The front line trenches were entirely taken by the Germans while the survivors fell back on the Stevens Redoubt complex (named after Brigadier-General G. A. Stevens) where, helped by a few men of the 18th Kings arriving from the rear lines, they held on until their ammunition was almost exhausted and they received orders to retire to Ham.

Another unit in General Maxse's XVIII Corps was the 61st Division. By the late evening of 21 March (see p.108), the 1/8th Argyll & Sutherland Highlanders had been able to protect this division's flank against enemy forces desperate to create more room for manoeuvre by breaking through on to the Saint Quentin - Vermand road; this had been achieved despite the failure of the counter-attack efforts of Colonel Dimmer and the 2/4th Royal Berkshires.

Now assisted by two companies of the 2/4th Royal Berkshires, the Argylls were ready once more to face enemy attack on the morning of 22 March. The attacks, each time following heavy bombardment, came at varying intervals from 8 a.m. onwards, with the Argylls holding their ground and the attacks repulsed. All seemed to be going well, while to the south the 2/5th Glosters were free from attack. There was a confident feeling that the defenders could hold their own.

Just after noon, however, orders came through to retire to new rear zone positions, some four miles back. This involved the successful movement of ammunition and guns, etc., and indeed in the course of this activity the 2/4th Royal Berkshires were able to recover some artillery pieces lost the previous day, 21 March. Some time later the actual withdrawal began, taking about two hours while rear parties covered the retreat. Once more, troops reaching new positions discovered the lack of trenches, for once again the Fifth Army's shortage of labour meant inadequate defences. With many entrenching tools lost in the recent fighting there was little prospect of quickly constructing new trenches.

During one of their attacks on the Argylls German troops had at last broken through between the British lines, at the junction of the Argylls' 183rd Brigade and the 2/5th Glosters' 184 Brigade. This opened the way for the enemy forces to begin a threatening advance south across the Saint Quentin - Vermand road through Holnon Wood and out into the area beyond. Low level German air attacks harassed the ground troops from all sides, although the defending British rifle and machine gun fire brought down one of the aircraft within the British lines. The pilot survived and was taken prisoner.

The defending troops, including the 2/5th Glosters, held off the attackers with strenuous efforts until XVIII Corps ordered a general retirement to the west. Around 2 p.m. on the afternoon of 22 March, therefore, a difficult fighting retreat began, back to a line of positions that stretched from about 2000 yards south-west of Vermand, near Villeveque and in front of Beauvais, to a similar distance west of Etreillers. The whole of the 61st Division was now on the move to the rear.

182 Brigade, consisting of two battalions of the Royal Warwickshire Regiment and the battle reserve survivors of the 2/8th Worcestershire Regiment, were the first to reach their new positions. 184 Brigade under Brigadier-General R. White, including the 2/5th Glosters, was ordered to retire soon after this, Brigade then deciding that the 2/5th Glosters should act as covering battalion during the Brigade's withdrawal towards Beauvois, acting in effect as rearguard to the whole of the 61st Division.

In the 24 hours from the moment when the Glosters first faced the enemy, at 5 a.m. on 21 March when they went into action in the Battle Zone near Holnon Wood, they had suffered under attacks from three German divisions and taken very heavy casualties as they fought to stem the German attack. Now, on 22 March, they were asked to undertake this rearguard action to cover the retirement of the rest of the Division. Fighting steadily over a distance of two miles, they reached their new positions in front of Beauvois at about 4 p.m. that day, joining the Corps front of nearly 21,000 yards - but their ordeal was not yet over.

Despite all efforts in the time available, little defence work had been achieved to dig trenches in the new positions. At around 5 p.m., therefore, General Maxse gave orders for yet another withdrawal, this time to the left bank of the Somme canal during the evening of 22 March.

At Beauvois the 9th Royal Scots, who had only just taken up their inadequate new position, had to withdraw from it to a point at Nesle, beyond the Somme canal. They were impressed by the German units' splendid display of force as they pursued the fighting withdrawal westwards. The immediate followers were skirmishers who indulged in minor actions from time time whenever the Royal Scots paused during their retreat - but behind them came numerous supporting infantry battalions, advancing in line and spread out wide across the battlefield. Like other British battalions, the Royal Scots could see that every path and road far to the rear of the enemy lines was packed with advancing German transport; the columns even included special vehicles fitted with winch mechanisms for their observation balloons to go aloft. Amidst the difficult conditions of their retreat the British units could not help admiring the staff work of the German army.

As part of the withdrawal General Gough sent instructions that the battalions forming the Corps' rearguard should hold on as long as possible: as soon as the 2/5th Glosters reached the new front line, for example, they were again given the task of forming the divisional rearguard and engaging the German troops that were now following close behind. By 10.30 p.m. on 22 March only the 2/5th Glosters remained; it was not until the early hours of 23 March that they managed to disengage and retire to the new lines beyond the Somme canal. Brigadier-General White, the Brigade Commander, was wounded during this action, and his Brigade Major taken prisoner.[5] The Major subsequently escaped while under escort near the German lines, when a chance explosion enabled him to get away and evade the pursuing fire as he dodged back to the British lines.

During the retreat the 2/5th Glosters, now down to a mere 150 men, were at Marcelcave with orders to dig in on the outskirts of the airfield. The Medical Aid Post here was overrun and the Medical Officer, Lieutenant Bernard J. Gallagher of the U.S. Army Medical Service, taken prisoner. Gallagher was one of several Americans at Saint Quentin with the British Army in March 1918, all originally from a party of 1500 medical doctors who joined the U.S. Army in 1917 and were almost immediately sent to the front as 'Yankee doctors' with battalions of the British Army in France. The British Fifth Army continued their retreat, eventually reaching Villers-Bretonneux some 40 miles west from Saint Quentin on the Roman road.

On 28 March, in what has been described as 'undeserved disgrace', General Sir Hubert Gough handed over his command to General Rawlinson and the Fifth Army was renamed the Fourth Army. A week later the German offensive was over, brought to a halt within nine miles of the crucial railhead of Amiens, but meanwhile Saint Quentin remained under German occupation; the Allies would not enter the city for several more months.

5. This was General White's second wound. 76 general officers became casualties in 1918, and total casualties among general officers for the whole of the First World War came to 232 – refuting the widespread notion that general officers were never seen in the front line.

Chapter Ten

THE TIDE TURNS

In August 1918 the Fourth Army occupied a sector of the front line between an east-west line on the map some two miles north of Albert and another, parallel with the Roman road from Amiens to Saint Quentin, about two miles south of the road at Villers-Bretonneux. Here they had the First French Army as their neighbours to the south.

For the French population of the German-occupied region there seemed no reason to suppose that the war might end soon. The people of Saint Quentin had been evacuated en masse in 1917 and the spring of 1918 had seen the great German advance westwards which almost broke through the Allied lines. On 8 August, however, the long-awaited Allied offensive began at 4.20 a.m., with the Australians and Canadians achieving sensational success. By the early afternoon most of the day's fighting was over, and by next morning the German High Command realised that it had suffered its greatest defeat since the beginning of the war, four long years ago. With some six German divisions overwhelmed by the British attack, General Erich Ludendorff called it 'the Black Day'.

From now on the German army would play a defensive role, in which the strong-points in front of Saint Quentin, and the Hindenburg Line itself, could be expected to play a vital part. Military tactics had changed since 1914, and the new technology and fresh thinking was in evidence during this crucial period.

No.201 R.A.F. Squadron, equipped with Sopwith Camel fighters temporarily operating as light bombers, was detailed to cooperate with the Australians as they advanced eastwards. At Proyart, some ten miles east of Villers-Bretonneux, a British aircraft (no doubt from this squadron) spotted a German railway gun coupled up to ammunition wagons and a locomotive with steam up; dropping a bomb, the pilot set part of the train on fire, an incident followed by the arrival of British cavalry from the 11th Hussars and 5th Dragoon Guards who engaged in fierce fighting with the soldiers manning the train. The German artillerymen were soon killed or captured, the cavalry squadrons moved off, leaving the train on fire - but men of the 8th Australian Field Company arrived, took over the train, put out the fires and drove the train into the British lines. This is widely believed to have been the

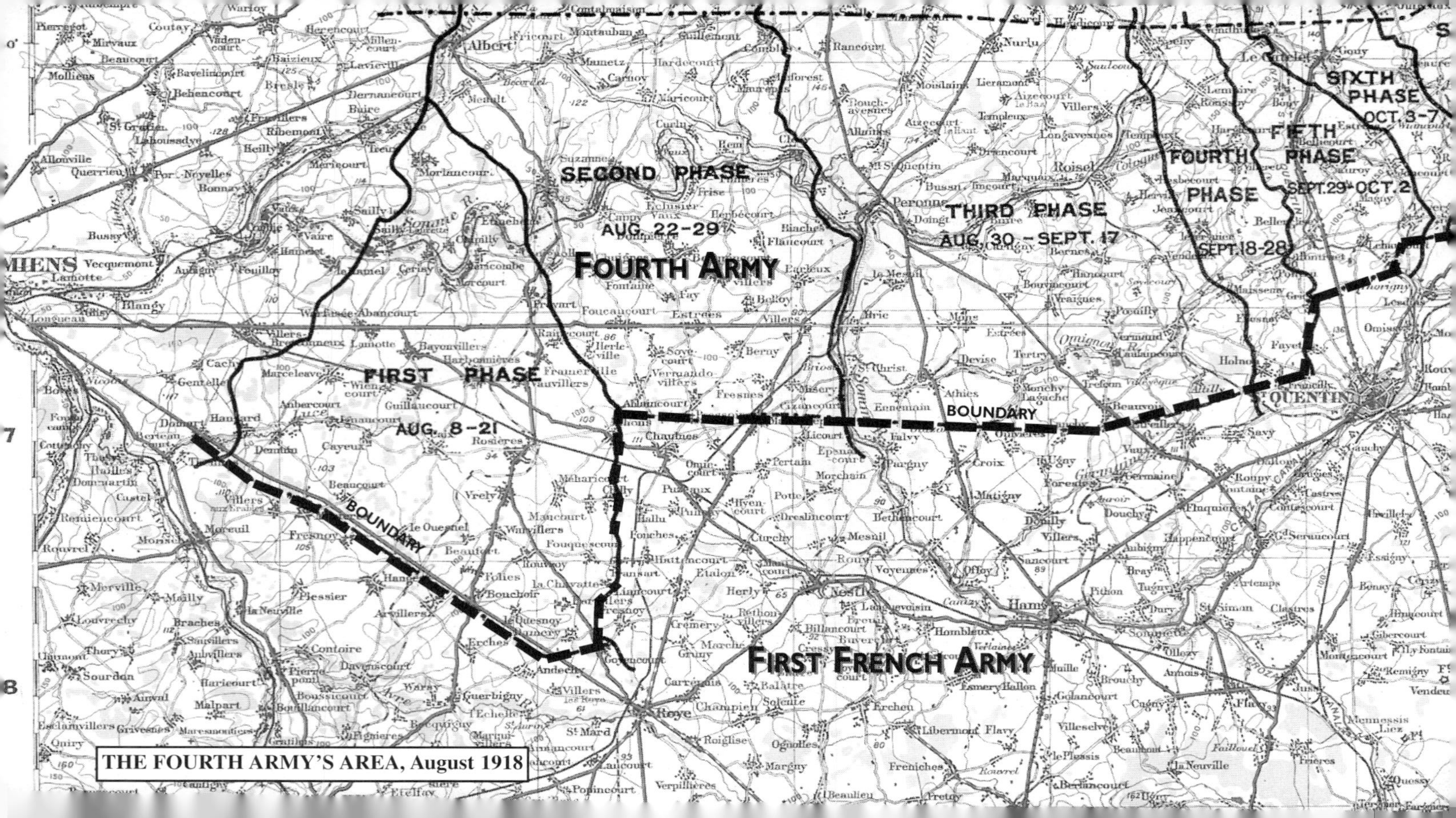

THE FOURTH ARMY'S AREA, August 1918

Holnon, pre-war. Destroyed before the German retreat to the Hindenburg Line in 1917, Holnon saw heavy fighting in March 1918 during the German offensive. It was recaptured during the Allied advance on Saint Quentin on 17 September by the 1st West Yorks, whose casualties here came to 234, including a high proportion of officers.

gun that was later taken to Paris by the Australians and put on display there.

All along the front line the German army was slowly being driven back, losing men and matériel all the time. The fighting was fierce, none the less, and the pursuing British, Australian and Canadian troops suffered many casualties.[6]

A typical unit at this time was the 2nd Manchesters, initially attached to the Canadian Corps of the Fourth Army. By coincidence the Battalion was back in the area it had occupied in March 1917 near Le Quesnoy and along the Amiens - Noyon road again, as in March 1917, in pursuit of the German army as it retreated to Saint Quentin. On 10 August 1918 they met stubborn enemy resistance at Damery Woods, about 1½ miles from Roye, and suffered a number of casualties.

The German successes of March 1918 had given the British Government a shock. General Gough's Fifth Army, which had been deprived of reinforcements despite the many trained men retained at regimental depots in the United Kingdom, now began to receive fresh drafts - between 21 March and the end of August more than half a million men were despatched to France. On 18 August a much-needed draft of 300 men reached the Manchesters and they now moved forward towards Harbonnières, south of the Roman road to Saint Quentin, to take over the line from an Australian battalion.

They hardly had time to settle in to their new positions before coming under a severe assault the next morning, in which they suffered

6. One of these was Major Marshall, the second in command, an intrepid character who was later described by the poet Wilfred Owen as 'Major Marshall of the ten wounds'. Marshall won the Victoria Cross in the engagement in which he was killed, while crossing the Sambre-Oise Canal on 4 November 1918.

nearly 100 casualties. Fighting continued for several days, until the German troops resumed their retreat eastwards. This pattern of almost unceasing attack and counter-attack became the norm for the whole Fourth Army for the next three weeks until, still in pursuit of the retreating enemy on 6 September, the Manchesters found themselves on familiar territory: the battalion reached the outskirts of Holnon Wood, not far from Manchester Hill outside Saint Quentin, the scene of their triumphs in April 1917.

The task of preparing to capture Saint Quentin, now a mere 3½ miles away, was passed to the men of the 1st and 6th Divisions (newly arrived from the Ypres Salient) and the 34th French Division. A week later the 32nd Division was relieved; the Manchesters moved back to La Neuville, near Corbie, to re-fit and prepare for their next move forward.

By 13 September the 1st South Wales Borderers, part of the 1st Division, had reached the outskirts of Vermand and then moved on to Bihecourt. They were returning through the villages along the River Omignon, ground lost a few months earlier at such cost to Gough's Fifth Army, and once again the casualties would be heavy. Two days later they reached the sunken road near Maissemy where RSM Brough and the men of the 1st North Staffs' Battalion HQ had fought so doggedly a few months earlier. Passing close to Maissemy, where Lieutenant-Colonel Le Fleming of the 9th East Surreys had been killed in March, the South Wales Borderers plunged into stiff fighting. By that evening the 1st Division's front line extended from Vadancourt through Maissemy to Holnon Wood.

After taking over from the 2nd Manchesters (32nd Division) on the outskirts of Holnon Wood, the 1st Gloucestershire Regiment stretched its line northwards from the wood to the right flank of the South Wales Borderers near Maissemy. Pressing forward with heavy artillery support, they captured Maissemy Ridge - at the cost of casualties that included the battalion medical officer, Lieutenant Birkett, RAMC. His replacement was killed almost immediately when a shell dropped on Battalion Headquarters. (It was during the operations here that the Glosters found a badly damaged field kitchen which had belonged to their sister battalion, the 2/6th Glosters, and had been abandoned by them during the March retreat.)

The villages of Holnon, Selency, Fresnoy-le-Petit, Pontruet and Sainte Hélène must all be recaptured before the occupying Germans could be expelled from Saint Quentin. This was a substantial task, the front to be attacked was some 7000 yards long, the Hindenburg Line

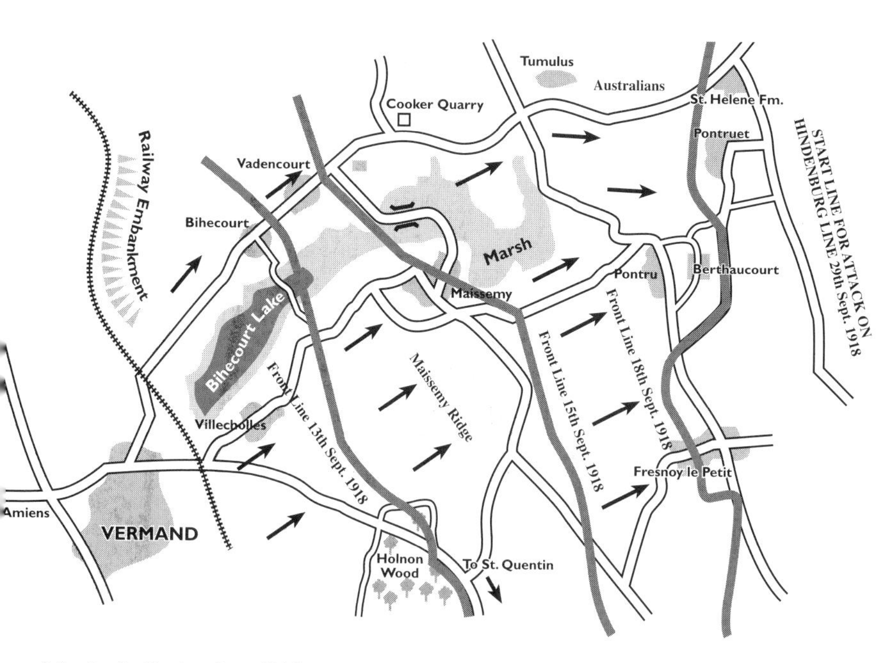

Attacks in September 1918, north of the Saint Quentin - Amiens road.

was not far off and the determined German defence of its outlying strong points led to some very stubborn fighting.

The date set for a major attack along the Fourth Army's sector in front of Saint Quentin was 18 September 1918. The 1st Division held the area north of the Roman road with the 6th Division south of the road and the French 34th Division beyond them in Etreillers. The familiar names of Savy village, Round Hill and Manchester Hill lay ahead.

Before the 6th Division could form up for the attack on 18 September, two days were needed to establish an assembly line - a task requiring care, for a mistake could be devastating. On this occasion one of the start lines was to be to the east of Holnon Wood, well in front of it, with a section of trench in Holnon village and joining the neighbouring 34th French Division. The work of clearing Holnon Wood was allocated to the 11th Essex which, despite an aggressive night attack on 17 September, were unable to take the wood until the next day. They then established a line of trenches facing Saint Quentin, while the 1st West Yorkshire was instructed to capture Holnon village. The R.A.F. carried out preliminary bombing attacks and tanks were ready to support the infantry.

Zero hour for 18 September was 5.20 a.m., but unfortunately the tanks were severely handicapped by heavy overnight rain which made the ground extremely slippery. The German response to the attack was brisk and divisions had difficulty in maintaining contact or receiving information, with senior officers frequently relying on runners or passing wounded.

The 1st and 6th Divisions overcame the stubborn resistance and reached many of their objectives for the day. In particular they made the crucial contact with the successful Australian brigade on the north flank of the 1st Division. The British troops were now capturing and advancing across areas that had been doggedly fought over six months earlier - Cooker Quarry, The Tumulus, the area near the Essling Redoubt which had seen much fighting by the North Staffs and West Kents. Fresnoy-le-Petit and 'the Quadrilateral', however, held out against the Allies as the 1/5th Gordons' stubborn defence at Fresnoy

The Quadrilateral. The former Enghien redoubt now (September 1918) extended by the Germans into a formidable strongpoint. First attacked on 18 September 1918, the position proved difficult to overcome. It was finally taken on 24 September by the combined efforts of the 11th Essex, 1st West Yorks, 1st Leicesters and the remaining companies of the 2nd Durhams.

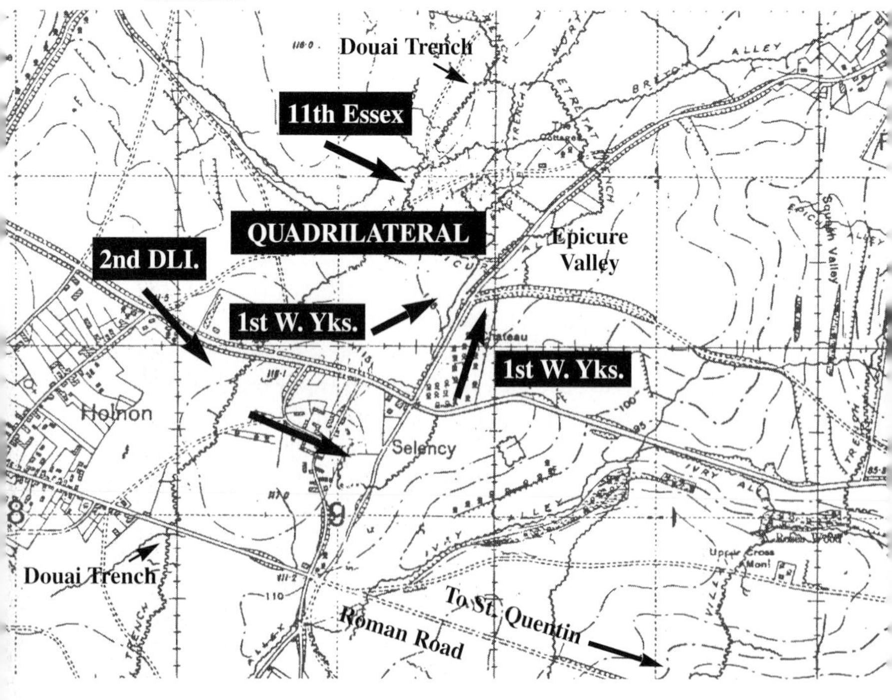

Redoubt on 21 March was repeated by the German troops. (The Quadrilateral was the new British name for the former Enghien Redoubt, now altered and strengthened by the Germans.)

Two scenes of bitter fighting in March 1918 overlooked Holnon - Round Hill and Manchester Hill, both now strongly garrisoned by the enemy. Capture of these two positions would protect Holnon from enemy fire during the assembly period, but the French division was unable to capture them and although the West Yorks finally captured most of the village by 17 September it was still not entirely satisfactory as an assembly point. None the less, it had to be used, despite the heavy cost in casualties (234 of the West Yorks, including a high proportion of officers, and heavy losses from the 2nd Durham Light Infantry, who were sent to assist).

The casualties were found to be inflicted from German positions on Round Hill in the French sector, which they had been unable to take and where the defenders had camouflaged their trenches with the abundant local growth of thistles.

Holnon Wood, meanwhile, was a considerable problem - with most of it drenched in gas and the tracks through it obliterated, the wood was virtually impassable. The two attacking brigades (71 and 16) therefore had to go round it. Despite these delays the 6th Division was ready alongside the 1st Division to go into the attack at 5.20 a.m. on 18 September. By the end of the day, after much heavy fighting, the British line had gained an advance of some 3000 yards and the capture of Saint Quentin seemed a little nearer.

Also on 18 September, men of 16 and 71 Brigades (6th Division) made a dawn attack on the strongly-held Quadrilateral, but were driven back by heavy artillery and machine gun fire. Of the two tanks detailed to assist, the 1st East Kents (16 Brigade) reported that one failed to start while the second sped away rapidly into Fresnoy-le-Petit - and was never seen again. To the right of the East Kents, men of the 1st Leicesters, 2nd Sherwood Foresters and 9th Norfolks (all in 71 Brigade) were held up and could not help 16 Brigade as planned. Casualties were heavy, with the 1st East Kents losing six officers and 150 men killed or wounded.

British camp in Holnon Wood

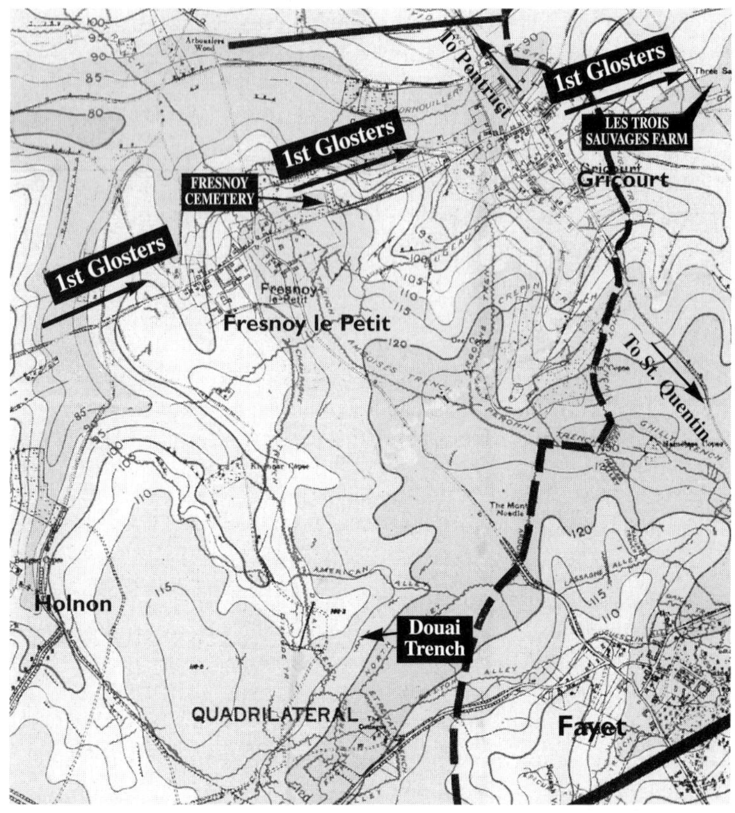

Fresnoy-le-Petit and Gricourt captured: on the morning of 24 September 1918, under a creeping barrage, the 1st Glosters went on the attack and after fierce fighting took Fresnoy cemetery but not the Redoubt there. During the afternoon they advanced to Gricourt and beyond to Les Trois Sauvages. Two platoons were later detached to deal with the strong point in Fresnoy village, which was still holding out but eventually surrendered by 10.30 p.m.

All the units became mingled together and were eventually formed into a composite battalion; this was used the next day, 19 September, for another attack on the Quadrilateral but the defending German troops were ready and after stiff fighting throughout the day the British were driven off.

During this second attack on the Quadrilateral on 19 September the 1st King's Shropshire Light Infantry managed to get into Fresnoy-le-Petit but, although they held it for some time, they were finally forced to retire. It was clear that the capture of the Quadrilateral was the true key to the whole advance on Saint Quentin, but this enhanced former

Fresnoy-le-Petit: a modern view of the cemetery, looking south. Attacking from the south and overcoming stubborn resistance, Fresnoy-le-Petit village (but not the German redoubt) was finally captured in the early hours of 24 September 1918 by the 1st Glosters and 2nd Welch. The defending Germans had their Battalion HQ in dugouts and tunnels in this cemetery and, owing to the intensity of the British barrage, failed to realise until too late that the Glosters were now outside the entrances. A judiciously placed pistol shot down one of the shafts quickly achieved the surrender of four officers and 160 other ranks sheltering below. A negotiated German surrender later that day finally cleared the enemy from the village.

British 'Enghien Redoubt' proved overwhelmingly difficult to take; first assumptions that it was being used for rearguard action only proved wrong as it became clear that the German defenders were prepared to stand their ground at all costs.

While the British troops now took a few days to reorganise, artillery rained down some 1000 shells a day into the Quadrilateral and on 24 September the 1st King's Shropshire Light Infantry (6th Division) were detailed to attack it yet again. Working with the 2nd York and Lancasters, they attacked it from the north and, making some progress, took 64 prisoners; but there was more to be done, and it was now the turn of 18 Brigade, also in the 6th Division, to make an attempt on it.

The Quadrilateral's defences included a long trench, known as Douai Trench, running north-east from in front of Holnon village across two roads leading west out of Saint Quentin, on to the Quadrilateral defences and then almost due north towards Fresnoy-le-Petit. The 1st West Yorks formed up just outside Holnon, in front of Douai trench. It was misty, and as the attack began some platoons lost direction. Four tanks, of which the West Yorks had great expectations, were quickly destroyed by enemy gunfire - a great loss. It therefore took almost two hours before the West Yorks and 11th Essex could establish some sort of footing in the enemy trenches, but they finally succeeded when the 11th Essex reached the north end of Douai trench and thence into the Quadrilateral itself. This involved them in some very stiff fighting and when they moved on to the southern end of the Quadrilateral, a position known as Epicure Valley, their numbers dwindled rapidly as they came under enemy fire from almost every direction.

The West Yorks had also encountered difficulties - together with the 2nd Durham Light Infantry they had been repulsed in several places along Douai trench. Two companies of the Durhams managed to force their way through the trench line and advance towards Saint Quentin, south of the main road and parallel with it; suffering heavy casualties, they were never seen again.

The Quadrilateral had still not been completely taken, yet if progress towards the Hindenburg Line was to be achieved it was essential to capture this stubbornly-held position quickly. On the evening of 24 September, therefore, yet another attack was mounted, this time with the support of the 1st Leicestershire Regiment. Success at last! The Leicesters, West Yorks and the remaining companies of the Durhams finally forced the surrender, despite heavy British casualties (particularly among battalion officers).

The French division to the south of Holnon Wood were also in action on 24 September. Round Hill fell to them that day, followed two days later by the capture of Manchester Hill. Remembering the events of April 1917 and March 1918 at these two sites, the Manchesters were delighted to hear that they were now both in Allied hands. Roupy, Savy and L'Epine de Dallon (where the 2nd Wiltshires had suffered so severely) were also recovered.

Further north along the line, a casualty of the Shropshires' unsuccessful attack on Fresnoy-le-Petit on 19 September crawled into the Battalion's front line during this period: this was Private Austin, who had been wounded three times, a member of B company which had engaged in bitter fighting in the attempt to take the village. He brought unhappy news - that the Germans had decided to shoot all the British wounded and that Austin had himself been fired on twice after calling for help.

It was time to renew the assault. At 5 a.m. on 24 September the 1st Division was instructed to attack Fresnoy, and the 1st Glosters, 2nd Welch Regiment and two companies of the South Wales Borderers finally captured the village which had resisted so stubbornly.

The German battalion headquarters in Fresnoy lay in very deep dug-outs in the cemetery, and such was the noise of the barrage that the enemy failed to realise the Glosters' presence - until a Very pistol fired down one of the shafts brought scores of men pouring out of another shaft. Four officers and some 160 Other Ranks were taken prisoner, together with many weapons and other booty including a supply of Iron Crosses. (The Glosters' regimental history comments somewhat light-heartedly that perhaps a ceremonial parade was in the offing.) The German commandant complained bitterly that his superiors' failure to warn him of the imminent attack had left his men sheltering underground instead of manning their trenches.

Maintaining their momentum and their success, the Glosters, Welch and Borderers moved on to the outskirts of Gricourt, one of the original objectives of the 18 September attack, taking more prisoners on their way. They then captured Gricourt itself, adding to the satisfaction of Brigadier-General Sir W. A. Kay.

A German counter-attack was now inevitable - and, sure enough, some two hours later scores of German troops poured out of the nearby trench system at Les Trois Sauvages Farm, supported by mortar fire. It was a very strong position and despite the repeated attacks of one battalion after another it had never been subdued in 1917. Even now it formed a distinct thorn in the side of the British troops at Gricourt, but although artillery fire was briefly considered the Glosters' intense rifle and machine-gun fire finally overcame the German assault.

Meanwhile, despite the capture of the village of Fresnoy and the German Battalion HQ, the strong-point there still held out and 90 per cent of the continuing British casualties came from its German snipers. The Glosters were running short of men to assault this difficult position, for most of the Battalion was heavily engaged beyond Gricourt. Two platoons of the Reserve Company remained, however, which were ordered to attack under Lieutenants Danahy and Gosling, the latter being wounded in the severe fighting.[7]

Whenever any of the German garrison attempted to surrender they were promptly shot down by their own men and the redoubt had still not fallen by 10.30 p.m. on 24 September; but some German soldiers managed to evade their own officers and reach the Glosters' trenches, one volunteered to return and persuade his comrades to surrender, and when the Glosters advanced shortly afterwards they encountered no opposition.

North of Gricourt, Pontruet and Sainte Hélène (marked on modern maps as Le Petit Arbre) remained to be taken, locations which in April

7. After the war Gosling was attached to a Russian regiment and in July 1919 was murdered by the Russians during a mutiny, some 300 miles to the south of Archangle. He is buried in the Allied cemetery in Archangel.

and May 1917 had kept two battalions of the Lancashire Fusiliers and the 23rd Manchesters fully engaged in their patrolling activity. The operation to take these two sites on 24 September 1918, by the 1/5th Lincolnshire Regiment assisting the 5th Leicesters and 6th Sherwood Foresters, was described as 'a minor operation'. It involved very intense fighting, however, particularly by the 5th Leicesters, in which Lieutenant J. C. Barrett won a Victoria Cross.

Both the 1st Northamptonshire Regiment and the 2nd Royal Sussex Regiment were involved in the fighting around Pontruet, their objective being the area by the modern Gricourt - Pontruet road and a sector about 2000 yards beyond.

At 5 a.m. on 24 September, the Northants and Royal Sussex went into the attack, passing near the site of the Essling Redoubt that the North Staffs. had defended so stoutly the previous March. They were helped by a creeping barrage and especially by the success of the Glosters, the Welch and the Borderers on their right flank, making such good progress towards Gricourt.

Unfortunately Pontruet did not fall. As a result, the German machine gunners, well sited in the south of the village, brought down devastating fire on the Northants' left flank and halted the advance. Tanks were called in but, as at the Quadrilateral, their contribution was inconsiderable - one never arrived, two others were destroyed by German artillery fire and the fourth became disorientated and disappeared completely towards Pontruet.

Meanwhile the Northants and Royal Sussex had reached their objective - but the heavy machine-gun fire from the German posts in Pontruet prevented them from holding it. They withdrew slightly to a

Fayet Château, pre-war. This elegant building was dynamited by the German Army in 1917 as part of the 'scorched earth' policy as they withdrew to the nearby Hindenburg Line. The very successful British assault on Fayet village, on 14 April 1917, included the capture of the ruins of the château by the 16th Highland Light Infantry in record time and played a major part in the British advance to the outskirts of Saint Quentin.

nearby trench. At about 11.30 a.m. a strong enemy force of some 400 men counter-attacked the remaining 80-odd men of the Royal Sussex A company who, under Captain H. Roberts, routed the attackers with a spirited bayonet charge.

Despite their numerous casualties, the Royal Sussex took 400 prisoners and two enemy guns, while the Northants' casualties totalled around 250 officers and men. The two weakened battalions expected a spell out of the line, but early the next day they were called on to support the neighbouring 2nd King's Royal Rifle Corps.

The strong enemy counter-attack was repulsed, with heavy enemy losses, and in the afternoon of 25 September the attackers withdrew. That evening, however, the Germans were in general retirement along the front, with the few parties of enemy troops in the area moving back into the formidable main defences of the Hindenburg Line.

The 2nd York and Lancasters were also engaged on 25 September. That morning they sent out a strong patrol near Fayet which returned with 107 German officers and men who had surrendered: morale was beginning to crumble in the German rank and file. Three days later a captured German soldier stated that he was a member of the last patrol covering the German withdrawal to the Hindenburg Line: he was not believed, but by 28 September it was impossible to contact the enemy. By next day, Lieutenant Lushington of the 1st East Kents and a large patrol were in possession of Fayet - and the liberation of Saint Quentin was at last in sight.

Fayet village, pre-war. Almost immediately after all the villagers were forced to leave, by 13 February 1917, the houses were destroyed so that they could not be used as shelter by the British army following the German retreat to the Saint Quentin defences. The 2nd Manchesters came down this road (towards the camera position) on 14 April 1917 on their way from Savy to attack Dancour trench. They took the road to the left, centre, which leads to Squash Valley.

By 28 September the Royal Sussex, the Northants and the rest of the 1st Division had been relieved from positions to the east of Gricourt, including posts near the notorious Trois Sauvages Farm. Now back in Vermand, the division began to prepare for the main attack on the Hindenburg Line the next day; all the Hindenburg Line outposts in the Saint Quentin area had now been captured or vacated.

This withdrawal enabled the 1st Division to take both Sainte Hélène and Pontruet, with the area beyond, as the start line for the Fourth Army's victorious attack on 29 September 1918.

It was now time for the 6th Division to move on - men of the 1st East Kents, 1st West Yorks and 1st Leicesters, for example, had all been engaged in strenuous fighting and the French army was waiting to take over. While momentous advances were under way to the north, therefore, they were relieved by the 4th French Division on the night of 29-30 September. The Division then enjoyed four days of rest before joining the advance eastwards, ending in the final victory some six weeks later.

The Hotel de Ville, Saint Quentin, at the Liberation. The Town Hall, showing its condition when the French under General Debeney entered the Place Hotel de Ville on 1 October 1918. Work began rapidly to clear up the debris...

...and work in progress.

Chapter Eleven

THE END AT LAST

The relief of Saint Quentin was about to begin, a momentous day that depended, as so often, on events elsewhere that opened the way for success.

The greatest contribution to the liberation of the city was probably the effort of the 46th (North Midland) Division which managed to cross the Saint Quentin canal in several places between Bellenglise and the Riqueval Bridge, and to break through the Hindenburg Line.

Of particular note was the exploit of nine men of the 1/6th Bn. North Staffordshire Regiment: attacking under Captain Charlton at 5.50 a.m. on 29 September 1918 in misty conditions, when they rushed the Riqueval Bridge over the canal before it could be destroyed. This contributed significantly to the impressive breakthrough by the 46th Division and the advance of nearly a mile beyond the canal, and by the evening of 29 September the British front line lay nearly 8000 yards beyond the Hindenburg Line. Here the 32nd Division was poised ready to attack Joncourt some 2000 yards further and then gain further ground.

The British army had been here before during this war - in 1914 great numbers of troops streamed down the road from Le Cateau, in retreat through Vermand or Saint Quentin: now, four years later, the

The canal, north of Saint Quentin: German engineers at Riqueval Bridge, preparing demolition charges for its destruction if capture threatened. Only the action by Captain Charlton and his men of 1/6th N. Staffs. on 29 September 1918 prevented this demolition.

The canal at Bellenglise. Note the barbed wire along the canal bank.

Allies were back, advancing. There was much to do, but it was becoming clear that the war would soon be over.

Although one French division, the 47th, was in action in the evening of 29 September, the French First Army had not been very active in the advance. As a consequence of the strong British assault north of the town when the British 46th Division successfully breached the

Bellenglise, showing British troops amongst some ruined buildings near the newly-captured village. It had formed part of the Hindenburg Line, so brilliantly broken by the 46th (North Midland) Division.

The Hotel de Ville, Saint Quentin, in 1918. Note the damage caused by British shelling.

German soldiers and French civilians. A photograph taken early in the German occupation. Many of the boys and men seen here would soon be required to work for the Germans, and some would be sent to Germany for this purpose.

Saint Quentin liberated, showing Allied progress during September 1918. By 29 September the Hindenburg Line had been breached near Bellenglise, forcing the Germans to retreat and evacuate Saint Quentin. On 1 October the French Army entered the city and took it back into French hands.

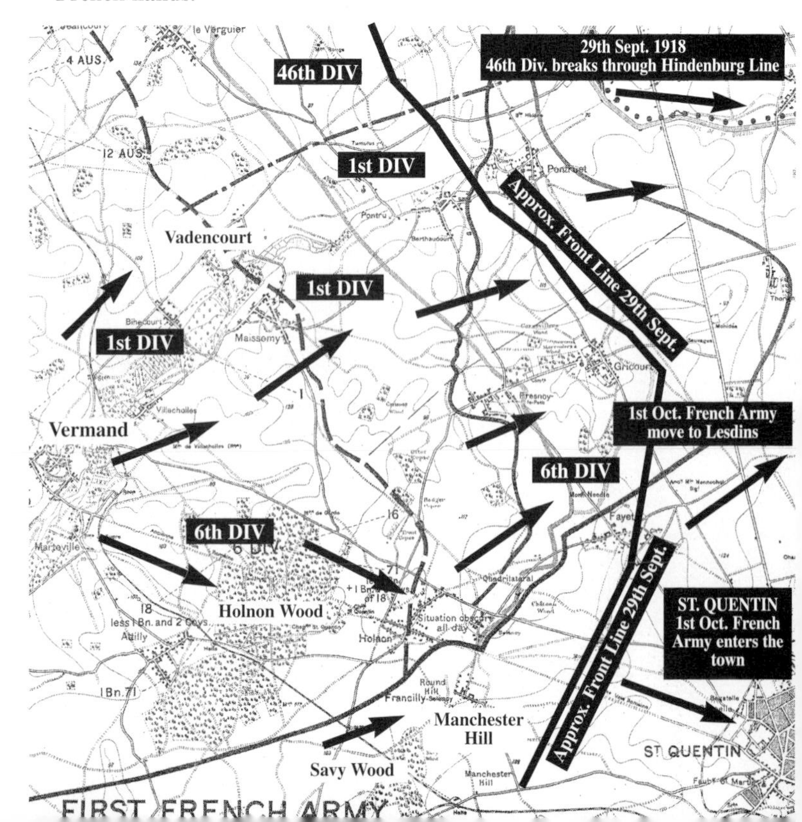

German prisoners of war at Saint Quentin railway station in 1918. It is not clear whether they are awaiting repatriation or despatch as a working party to clear the battlefields.

Hindenburg Line at Bellenglise, the occupying Germans had been forced to evacuate the city. Leaving it empty, much of it now in ruins, they withdrew to the rear: by 1 October the French 401st Infantry Regiment was able to enter the now-deserted city of Saint Quentin before pushing on to the Saint Quentin canal between Le Tronquoy and Lesdins by 2 October. By 19 October, the 153rd French Infantry Division had crossed the River Oise and liberated Hamégicourt and Brissy; after strenuous fighting, other villages were taken, the 168th

Saint Quentin Cathedral, 1919. The basilica first suffered serious damage in April 1917 when the British destroyed its spire, which had been used as a German observation post. Further damage continued in 1918 during the various attempts by the British and French to capture the city.

The Rue d'Isle, Saint Quentin, 1919 and 1999. Ruins in March 1919 and a modern shot taken from the Place 8 Octobre, with the canal and railway station behind the camera. In August 1914 the German cavalry rode up this hill to the Cathedral and the Hotel de Ville in the city centre.

Saint Quentin under bomardment in August 1917.

Infantry Division crossed the river north-east of Saint Quentin and early on 25 October the 418th and 79th Infantry Regiments, supported by light tanks, broke through German defences. The whole area around Saint Quentin was finally and fully liberated on 27 October.

Although the Armistice brought peace, Saint Quentin needed its people back again, houses and commerce needed to be rebuilt, lives had to be resumed. It was an immense task, for not a village around it was intact - the devastation throughout in the area was overwhelming. It was said, for example, that it was possible to travel from Soissons to Saint Quentin without seeing a single undamaged house. The construction of the Hindenburg Line and the bitter fighting in 1917 and 1918 had brought devastation to many of the villages described here - Vermand, Fayet, Savy, Roupy - and more. Many of their residents would never return, victims of the fighting or better suited elsewhere after being thrown out of their homes in February 1917. The majority did return, however, to work hard at reconstructing their lives and their homes.

History and geography are perennial factors in the life of communities and in 1940 history was to repeat itself. Saint Quentin came under threat once again as the French army, fighting strongly, was driven back by overwhelming invading German forces. On 18 May the Panzer troops entered the city and another four-year period of occupation began.

Chapter Twelve

ST. QUENTIN TOURS

Maps needed: the most satisfactory map for visiting the whole area around Saint Quentin is the Institut Geographique National (IGN) green series (Scale l:100,000), No 4 Laon/Arras.

TOUR No 1

Because the battlefield was the scene of stirring events, not only when the 2nd Manchesters were here in April 1917, but also in August 1914 and again in March and September 1918, the area around Savy is particularly interesting. Within a time-scale of less than one year, two men - Major Lumsden in 1917 and Lieutenant-Colonel Elstob in 1918 - won the Victoria Cross in actions within a few hundred yards of each other near the little village of Francilly-Selency, the objective of the 2nd Manchesters on 2nd April 1917.

A good place to start the tour is on the N 29 just east of Vermand, a village about 3 miles from the St.Quentin motorway exit (Junction 10). Coming-out of Saint Quentin, turn left just before Vermand on to the D 73, continue along it to Villeveque and just beyond this village turn left on to the D733 leading to Etreillers. Across the fields, looking half-right, the village of Beauvois is visible in the distance: this was where the 2nd Manchesters had their HQ in 1917 before moving to the front line near Savy Wood.

Bear right in Etreillers on the D33 to the cross-road junction with the D32 and turn left along it towards Roupy. On the right of the road, almost immediately, you will see a retirement home in a clump of trees: this is the Château de Pommery, where on 2 April 1917 the 2nd Manchesters formed up, ready to depart for their attack on Francilly-Selency. Nearly a year later, a sister battalion, the 17th Manchesters, fought in the château grounds on 21 March 1918 as the garrison of what was then called Goodman Redoubt.

The fields on the left-hand side of the D32 mark the ground over which the 2nd Manchesters went forward on the 2nd April 1917 towards Savy (which is visible in the distance) on their way to the start line ready for their attack. At the Roupy cross-roads turn left towards St.Quentin on to the busy D 930. In the angle between these two roads was the site of another redoubt in the chain of the 1918 defences. Known as Stanley Redoubt, it was manned by the 19th Battalion

King's Liverpools on 22nd March 1918. On the 27th August 1914 British troops, including Major Tom Bridges and his Dragoon Guards, passed through Roupy village in their retreat from Mons.

About 100 yards from the cross-roads, turn left off the D930 St.Quentin road into the village of Roupy and go forward past the church on the right (beware speed bumps in the road). Beyond the houses, the communal cemetery next to a sharp right-hand bend in the road contains the graves of several British casualties from the fighting here.

Holding a line of trench just behind this cemetery on 22 March 1918, a platoon of the 19th King's Liverpools made a desperate but vain attempt to stop the advancing Germans before being overwhelmed and the few survivors captured.

As you continue along this road you will approach Savy and, just before the village on the left-hand side of the road, Savy British Cemetery containing some 800 graves. Carry on from it to the T junction, turn right then almost immediately left to another T junction. Turn right here on to the D681, which quickly brings you to the edge of Savy village. On 1 April 1917 the 11th (Lonsdale) Battalion of the Border Regiment, who had been given the task of capturing the village, reached the trench line here by 6.30 a.m. It was also the start line for the next phase of the advance undertaken by two battalions of the Lancashire Fusiliers.

Continue on the Holnon road, the D681. In the fields to the right of this road, the 15th and 16th Battalions of the Lancashire Fusiliers suffered heavy casualties on 1 April 1917 as they advanced to capture the railway line across the battlefield immediately in front of them. The railway line connected St. Quentin with Vermand via a junction called 'The Halte'; the remains of the line and its embankment can be seen from the prominent gas installation on the right of the road about half a mile from Savy. (This is marked on the map as "Poste Gaz".)

Leave the car and walk eastwards along the former permanent way towards the woods. Looking out over the fields to your right, you will get some idea of the formidable task that faced the attacking Lancashire Fusiliers in April 1917.[8]

The 2nd Manchesters were to undertake the next advance. At dawn on 2 April 1917 they left the railway embankment and moved into the attack, striking northwards towards Holnon with the village of Francilly-Selency as their objective, located to the right of Round Hill. (Thus named by the British, the small hill was a German strong-point. It is visible to the left of the embankment looking towards Holnon.)

8. At the time of going to press (Autumn 2000), road-works for the updated link road to Amiens appear to threaten this site. The new road may give a fresh view of Savy Wood and surviving lengths of railway embankment.

Looking eastwards along the railway line towards the wood, another hillock, called Manchester Hill, can just be seen, with a railway junction, "The Halte", close to it. It was the 2nd Manchesters' capture of this high ground that earned it its British name. Despite the fact that both Manchester Hill and Round Hill were very strongly held, the Manchesters eventually captured Francilly-Selency together with a battery of German guns just outside the village.

Return to the car at 'Poste Gaz' and travel towards Holnon still on the D681, bearing right at the junction. At the cross-roads in Holnon take a sharp turn to the right.This leads to Francilly-Selency; when you reach the cross-roads there, take another turn to the right on to the D683 and into the village itself. By the Mairie, stop and look at the Memorial to the Manchesters - 2nd and 16th Battalions - who fought here in 1917 and 1918 respectively. Their capture of the battery of German guns in 1917 was achieved in the fields a few hundred yards opposite the Mairie and it was the ultimate recovery of the guns that earned Major Lumsden, R.M.Artillery, his Victoria Cross..

Return to the car. As you continue southwards along the D683 you will see, almost immediately on the right of the road, a clump of trees on a small hillock; this marks the remains of the Manchester Redoubt, (usually called Manchester Hill), part of the defence line of redoubts set up in 1918. It was here, of course, that Lieutenant-Colonel Elstob of the 16th Manchesters won his V.C. on 21 March 1918. He has no known grave but must lie close by the Redoubt where he was buried by the Germans.

Turn right at the T junction on to the D68 and stop beside the adjacent farm for a much closer look at the former redoubt. If crops permit, it is worth walking along the side of the line of trees, then bearing to the right and going forward to a wooden post which (usually) has a rubber tyre on top: this marks the former observation post of the redoubt.

Return to the car and continue a short way along the D68, bringing you almost immediately to "The Halte". Although the railway track has long since been removed the remains of its route crossing the road and the nearby railway station are clearly visible. Enemy fire from here on 1 April 1917 held up the advance of the Lancashire Fusiliers. It is interesting to take the field path, across the road from"The Halte", and pause after about 250 yards: the all-round view from here reveals the scale of the task facing the Lancashire Fusiliers and Manchesters in order to gain the capture of Francilly-Selency.

On 13 April 1917 the 2nd Manchesters were instructed to attack a trench to the north-west of St. Quentin. To follow in their footsteps, leave Manchester Hill via Francilly-Selency and make for the main St.Quentin road, the N.29.

Turn right along this road. (You are now in the area where in September 1918 the 1st West Yorks fought to establish a Start Line for the British advance on St.Quentin.) Within about 200 yards, just before the road bears left and descends into St.Quentin, take a sharp turn to the left, on a narrow road that runs alongside a clump of trees. As the road bends slightly to the right, observe some waste building material on the left-hand side of the road. This was the Enghien Redoubt, another of the 1918 line of redoubts and garrisoned in the spring of that year by a detachment of the Ox. & Bucks.L.I. (Later, it was extended by the Germans and named 'The Quadrilateral' by the British.)

Cross over the bridge which spans the motorway and descend into the village of Fayet. Immediately, take a very sharp turn back to the right; at the end of this short road you face the field, known to the Manchesters as Squash Valley, where they rested before continuing to their assembly position. Turn left up-hill and take the next turn on the right, along a ridge through a short row of modern houses. Stop the car beyond the final house.

Squash Valley lies down to the right, with a small copse called Fig Wood on the left. The Manchesters came up to this crest, then descended through Fig Wood to the other side into what is now a busy shopping and commercial centre. Reverse direction, turn right at the junction and then right again, out of the housing estate on to the D58.

In the open ground here you are in the sector which was involved in heavy fighting in September 1918: on 25 September a strong patrol of the 2nd York & Lancasters captured 107 German Officers and men, almost the last German troops to be captured before they evacuated St.Quentin a few days later.

The shopping centre is quickly visible on the right - the area where the 2nd Manchesters formed up in April 1917 for their attack up the shallow valley to your left. Carry on for a short distance into housing once more, turn left into the Rue de Lille and follow it to the T junction at the top. Turn left here on to the D732, continue for a few hundred yards and stop by the field on the right hand side of the road with a view back down the valley, just before the next cross-roads. This was the site of Dancour Trench, the objective gained by the 2nd Manchesters on 14 April 1918. Looking back across the road and down to the Manchesters' assembly point in the modern shopping centre, the difficult approach up-hill can be clearly seen and appreciated.

TOUR No 2.

Take the N44 heading north out of St.Quentin and after about 11 kilometres stop at the junction of this road with the D932 (sign-posted Le Cateau). Park on the right of the N44, cross it and walk about 50 yards up the lane to the Riqueval Bridge spanning the St Quentin Canal. This bridge was used in one of the routes taken by troops during the Mons Retreat in 1914, and on 29 September 1918 Captain Charlton and nine of his men from 1/6th North Staffs. succeeded in capturing the bridge before it could be destroyed. Return to the car.

Back on the N44 again, drive south towards St.Quentin but after about a mile take the D33 road to the right into Bellenglise. Cross the bridge over the canal: this was another section crossed by the 46th (North Midland) Division on 29 September 1918. Almost immediately beyond Bellenglise, you will reach a T junction marked on the map as Le Petit Arbre and known to the British as Ste. Hélène Farm. Turn left on to the D732 to go into Pontruet. It was near here that Lieutenant Barrett with the 5th Leicestershires won his V.C. on 24th September 1918.

In Pontruet turn right on to the D 73, then in Pontru turn left along the D 57. Pause at the Water Tower - it was near here that a company of the 1st North Staffs occupied a strong point known as the Essling Redoubt in March 1918. Continue to Fresnoy le Petit where the 1/5th Gordon Highlanders were in action on 21 March 1918. Turn left at the cross-roads and continue as far as the cemetery on the left hand side of the road. In September 1918 the Germans had made deep dug-outs in the cemetery to accommodate a Battalion Headquarters and the eventual capture of this position and the nearby strong point caused the 1st Glosters many casualties.

Carry on to Gricourt, turn right at the cross-roads on to the D 732 then sharply to the left along a narrow lane. Stop when you can see the motorway in the near distance: a German sector near here, known as Les Trois Sauvages, was the scene of many clashes between the British and the German troops holding the area in both 1917 and 1918.

Reverse direction, return to the D 732 and turn right along it through Pontruet to the junction at Le Petit Arbre. The British front line of March 1918 ran almost parallel on the left hand side of the D 732 at this point. It was part of the 2000 yards of front that the 1st North Staffs were appalled to learn they were expected to occupy when they took over in March 1918. Turn left at Le Petit Arbre, on to the D 31. A striking feature to the right, just over a mile along the road, is 'The

Tumulus', cone-shaped and tree-topped, which was used by the British as a signalling platform during the March retreat. The area to the left of the road was the scene of the 8th West Kents' fighting retreat on 21-22 March 1918; the land on the right of the road was fought over by the 3rd Rifle Brigade. Continue forward when the road crosses the D 57 and is re-designated the D33.

Shortly afterwards (about 1/4 mile) the German cemetery comes into view and almost immediately on the right hand side a small track marks the location of Cooker Quarry. A few yards further on and to the left is Vadancourt Chateau, made into a fortified Battalion HQ by the 8th West Kents when the Fifth Army took over the area in 1918.

Lieutenant-Colonel Dimmer is buried in Vadancourt Commonwealth War Graves cemetery, easily found beside the road in the village itself. Moving on, the next village is Bihecourt where Ivor Gurney was wounded during an attack by his battalion (2/5th Glosters) on 7-/8 April 1917. It was along this road that the 8th West Kents retreated on 22 March 1918 towards Vermand, suffering the minimum of casualties even though dense barbed-wire entanglements prevented them from using the fields on each side of the road as escape routes.

The road crosses the track of the former St.Quentin to Roisel railway, and the old railway embankment can be seen here to the right. This embankment was where the 2/5th Glosters took post prior to their attack on Bihecourt 7-8 April 1917 in which the Battalion suffered nearly 50 casualties.

Enter Vermand, a place well known to the British at various times in 1914, 1917 and 1918. At the junction with the main road, the N 29, turn left towards St.Quentin and take the next road on the left (after about 200 yards), the D 73 to Villecholles. Carry on to Maissemy and enter the village, continuing to the fork in the road where the D735 should be taken. It was along this sunken road that the 1st North Staffs held out at their Battalion HQ. and RSM Brough D.C.M. seized a rifle and picked off the attacking Germans one by one.

As you continue forward, the main N 29 soon comes into view. The ground on the left hand side of the road is where Lieutenant-Colonel Dimmer V.C. was shot down on 21 March 1918 as he rode forward at the head of his men. Turn left along the N29 towards St.Quentin. Holnon Wood lies on your right; the 2/5th Glosters were in action just in front of it during the German March Offensive.

TOUR No 3.

Approaching Saint Quentin along the N 29, go past the motorway access road, and continue straight ahead towards St.Quentin, passing the large French military cemetery on the left beside the first of two roundabouts about half a mile apart. (Just beyond the second one, a small road to the right is sign-posted to the German military cemetery, with its impressive memorial.)

Continue straight ahead and ignore signs for the city centre leading off to the right. Go forward beneath the flyover into the city and, a few hundred yards further on, across the St.Quentin canal. Follow signs to Laon (but ignore a right fork to Laon on the D8 road) until you reach a large roundabout and turn right on to the N44 signposted La Fère and Laon. After about 1½ miles, note the wood on the left hand side of the road, known to the British army as Sphinx Wood; opposite it, at Le Pontchu Quarry on the right of the road, Captain Johnston and his men stood their ground during the enemy attacks of 21 March 1918.

At the next crossroads turn right on to the D 576 (signposted Urvillers and Essigny) and continue straight through Urvillers to Essigny-Le-Grand. Both were places which were heavily involved in the March 1918 fighting. At Essigny-Le-Grand turn left on to the D 8 and almost immediately turn right on to the D 72 signposted Seraucourt-le-Grand. In about a mile, after crossing the railway line, the road meets a slight incline and it was here on the higher ground that Station Redoubt was located. Continuing along the D72 note the British Cemetery of Grand Seraucourt on the right of the road as the road turns sharply to the left (access via one-way circuit through the village) and continue along the D 72 through two right-angled bends into the village. From these two bends go across the crossroads and bear right at the fork beyond, signposted Contescourt, D 32. Pass through Contescourt and in about one mile the D 1040 leads left to Castres. Ignore this turn and continue until, after about half a mile, you find the a minor road to the left to Giffécourt. Turn into it: the high ground ahead was the site of the Boadicea Redoubt manned by the 2nd Royal Inniskillings on 21 March 1918.

Continue into Giffécourt. At the T-junction turn left into Castres, then left on to the D 1040 again, back to the D 321, and turn left again. This takes you into Grugies: turn right at the crossroads, passing under the railway bridge. The sharp bend at the bridge was the site of Racecourse Redoubt where Second Lieutenant De Wind of the 15th Royal Irish Rifles won his V.C. on 21 March 1918.

Reverse direction and go through Grugies along the D 671, under the motorway and into Gauchy, where you turn left almost immediately on to the D 678 signposted Dallon. Continue forward, cross over the canal, go up-hill (ignore the D 67 road) and at the D 930 turn left, signposted Ham.

Cross over the motorway and enter L'Epine de Dallon, a hamlet on the brow of the hill. The redoubt here was held by the 2nd Wiltshires on 21 March 1918. Continue forward into Roupy and the site of the Stanley Redoubt at the crossroads in March 1918.

To continue the tour, carry on down the D 930 and turn left turn left on to the D 56 leading to Bray St.-Christophe and thence continue on the D 34 to Tugny-et-Pont. Following this road through the village stop at the bridge at Pont de Tugny, for it is here that Lieutenant C.L.Knox of the Royal Engineers won his V.C. for his part in the destruction of the bridge spanning the canal on 22nd March 1918. Continue right on the D34 to St.Simon. In the village take a left turn on to the D 32 which leads through Artemps and thence to Seraucourt-le-Grand and by the D321 to St, Quentin.

WALK

In 1914, two soldiers, Pte Thomas Hands, 1st King's Own and Pte John Hughes 2nd R.Irish Rifles, were left behind in St. Quentin. Taken in by French civilians, they were kept safe until they were denounced by a French woman, tried and then shot by the Germans. They are buried in St.Quentin Northern Communal Cemetery in Rue Georges Pompidou where their graves are next to each other in Plot 19, Row E - Graves 10 and 11. It is not difficult to reach the cemetery and these graves, which presumably receive few British visitors.

Follow the Rue Georges Pompidou, the D8 to Bohain, leading north out of the city centre. The extensive town cemetery is clearly visible on the right after about half a mile and the plots inside are well indicated by numbered posts.

BIBLIOGRAPHY

The History of The Cheshire Regiment in the Great War, Crookenden, Chester, nd.
Regimental Records of the Royal Welch Fusiliers (late the 23rd Foot), 1914-1918 (France & Flanders), Foster Groom & Co. London.
The History of The Lincolnshire Regiment 1914-1918 Simpson. Medici Society. London 1931.
History of the Dorsetshire Regiment 1914-1919 Ling, Dorchester. 1932

History of the East Surrey Regiment Pearse & Sloman. Vols II (1914-1917) & Vol III (1917-1919) Medici Society, London 1925
The Worcestershire Regiment in The Great War Stacke. 1928
The Diehards in The Great War. A History of the Duke of Cambridge's Own (Middlesex Regt.) 1914-1919 Wyrall Vol. I, 1914-1916, Vol. II, 1916-1919 Harrison. London. 1926
The History of The Duke of Cornwall's Light Infantry 1914-1919 Wyrall. Methuen. 1932.
The Queen's Own Royal West Kent Regt. 1914-1919 Atkinson. Simpkin, Marshall, Hamilton, Kent. London. 1924
The Royal Scots 1914-1919 Ewing. Oliver & Boyd. London. 1925. Volumes 1 & 2.
The History of The Suffolk Regiment 1914-1927 Murphy. Hutchinson & Co. London. 1928.
History of The East Lancashire Regiment in The Great War 1914-1918, Littlebury Bros Ltd. Liverpool, 1936
The Manchester City Battalions Book of Honour Eds. Kempster and Westropp. Sherratt and Hughes. London. 1917.
History of the Manchester Regt. (Late the 63rd and 96th Foot) H.C.Wylly. 1925.
Sixteenth, Seventeenth, Eighteenth, Nineteenth Battalions The Manchester Regt. (First City Bde.) A Record 1914-1918 Sherratt & Hughes Manchester 1923.
The Border Regiment in The Great War Wylly. Gale & Polden, Aldershot 1924
The Story of the 2/5th Battalion The Gloucestershire Regt. 1914-1918 Barnes Gloucester.1930
History of The 15th Battalion The Highland Light Infantry (City of Glasgow Regiment) Chalmers. McCallum & Co. Glasgow. 1934
History of the 16th Battalion The Highland Light Infantry (City of Glasgow Regiment) Chalmers. McCallum & Co. Glasgow. 1930
The Gordon Highlanders in the First World War C.Falls. University Press, Aberdeen. 1958
The History of the Lancashire Fusiliers 1914-1918 Latter. Gale & Polden. Aldershot. 1949
Terriers in the Trenches: The History of the Post Office Rifles Messenger. Picton Publishing. 1982
The 16th Foot. A History of The Bedfordshire and Hertfordshire Regiment Maurice. Constable & Co.Ltd. London. 1931
History of the 1st & 2nd Battalions The North Staffordshire Regiment 1914-1923 Hughes & Harber Ltd. Longton, Staffs. 1923
A Short History of the Sixth Division. Aug. 1914-March 1919 Marden. Hugh Rees Ltd. London. 1920
Artillery & Trench Mortar Memories 32nd Division Various. Unwin Bros.London & Woking. 1932
The History of The 35th Division in the Great War Davson. Sifton Praed & Co. London. 1926

The History of the 36th (Ulster) Division C.Falls. McCaw, Stevenson & Orr Ltd. London. 1922
History of The Royal Regiment of Artillery. Western Front 1914-18 Gen. Sir Martin Farndale. RA Instituition. 1986
On The Road from Mons Clifton-Shelton Hurst & Blackett Ltd. London 1917
Forty Days in 1914 Maj.Gen. Sir F.Maurice. Constable & Co. Ltd. London. 1919
My Bit Ed. Richard Holmes. Crowood Press, Ramsbury, Wilts.
The Memoirs of Field-Marshal The Viscount Montgomery of Alamein K.G Collins, London, 1958
Official History of the Great War. Military Operations France and Belgium 1918 Edmonds. Macmillan & Co Ltd. London 1935
Official History of The War. The War in The Air. Vol. IV H.A.Jones. Oxford, Clarendon Press. 1934.
Dishonoured, Peter T. Scott. Tom Donovan, London, 1994
The Sky Their Battlefield T.Henshaw. Grub Street, London SW11 1HT. 1995.
Above The Trenches Shores, Franks & Guest. Grub Street, London SW11.1HT 1990
The Fifth Army in March 1918 W.Shaw Sparrow. The Bodley Head. London. 1921
The Fifth Army Gen. Sir H.Gough. Hodder & Stoughton London. 1931
The March Retreat Gen. Sir Hubert Gough. Cassell & Co Ltd. London. 1934
Manchester Pals. A History of The Two Manchester Brigades Michael Stedman. Leo Cooper, London. 1994
Liverpool Pals. A History of the 17th, 18th,19th and 20th (Service) Battalions The King's (LiverpoolRegiment) 1914-1919 Graham Maddocks. Leo Cooper. London. 1991
Wilfrith Elstob V.C., D.S.O., M.C Robert A.Bonner. Fleur de Lys Publishing, Knutsford. 1998
The Kaiser's Battle Martin Middlebrook. Alan Lane Penguin Books Ltd. London. 1978
'The Story of The Fourth Army' in *The Battles of The Hundred Days* Montgomery. Hodder & Stoughton Ltd. London. 1919.
No Man's Land John Toland. Book Club Associates. London. 1980
The Paris Gun H.W.Miller. Geo. G.Harrap & Co. Ltd. London/1930
Great Battles of World War 1 A.Livesey. Michael Joseph, London. 1989
On the Trail of The Poets of The Great War - Wilfred Owen McPhail & Guest. Leo Cooper. 1998
Ivor Gurney War letters, Ed R.K.R.Thornton. Hogarth Press, London 1984
Far From A Donkey. The Life of General Sir Ivor Maxse John Baynes. Brassey's (UK) Ltd. 1995
Douglas Haig. The Educated Soldier John Terraine. Leo Cooper. London. 1990.
The Register of The Victoria Cross This England. 1988.
British Regiments 1914-18 E.A.James. Samson Books, London.1978.
Sur les traces de la Grande Guerre dans la région de Saint-Quentin, Michel

Dutoit, Comité de Bassin d'Emploi, Saint Quentin, 2000
Sous la Botte, Histoire de la ville de Saint-Quentin pendant l'occupation allemande, Elie Fleury, Saint Quentin, 1925
1914 - 1918 La Grande Guerre vécue - racontée - illustrée par les combattants, (2 vols.), ed. Christian Froge. Librairie Aristide Quillet, Paris, 1922
1914 - 1919 *L'Album de la Guerre,* (2 vols.) L'Illustration, Paris, 1924

INFANTRY BATTALIONS INVOLVED IN BATTLE AT SAINT QUENTIN, 1917 and 1918

1st DIVISION
1st Brigade: 1st Black Watch, 1st Loyal North Lancashire Regiment, 1st Cameron Highlanders
2nd Brigade: 2nd Royal Sussex Regiment, 1st Northamptonshire Regiment, 2nd King's Royal Rifle Corps
3rd Brigade: 1st South Wales Borderers, 1st Gloucestershire Regiment, 2nd Welch Regiment
6th DIVISION
16th Brigade: 1st East Kent Regiment, 1st King's Shropshire Light Infantry, 2nd York & Lancaster Regiment
18th Brigade: 1st West Yorkshire Regiment, 2nd Durham Light Infantry, 11th Essex Regiment
71st Brigade: 1st Leicestershire Regiment, 2nd Sherwood Foresters, 9th Norfolk Regiment
24th DIVISION (part)
17th Brigade: 3rd Rifle Brigade
72nd Brigade: 9th East Surrey Regiment, 8th Royal West Kent Regiment, 1st North Staffordshire Regiment
30th DIVISION
21st Brigade: 2nd Green Howards, 2nd Wiltshire Regiment, 17th Manchester Regiment
89th Brigade: 17th, 18th and 19th King's Liverpool Regiment
90th Brigade: 2nd Bedfordshire Regiment, 2nd Royal Scots Fusiliers, 16th Manchester Regiment
32nd DIVISION
14th Brigade: 5/6th Royal Scots, 1st Dorsetshire Regiment, 15th Highland Light Infantry, 2nd Manchester Regiment
96th Brigade: 15th and 16th Lancashire Fusiliers, 16th Northumberland Fusiliers
97th Brigade: 11th Border Regiment, 1/5th Border Regiment, 2nd King's Own Yorkshire Light Infantry, 10th Argyll & Sutherland Highlanders, 16th and 17th Highland Light Infantry
35th DIVISION
104th Brigade: 17th, 18th and 20th Lancashire Fusiliers, 23rd Manchester Regiment

105th Brigade: 15th and 16th Cheshire Regiment, 15th Sherwood Foresters, 14th Gloucester Regiment
106th Brigade: 17th West Yorkshire Regiment, 17th Royal Scots, 19th Durham Light Infantry, 18th Highland Light Infantry

36th (ULSTER) DIVISION

107th Brigade: 1st, 2nd and 15th Royal Irish Rifles
108th Brigade: 12th Royal Irish Rifles, 1st and 9th Royal Irish Fusiliers
109th Brigade: 1st, 2nd and 9th Royal Inniskilling Fusiliers

61st DIVISION

182nd Brigade: 2/6th and 2/7th Royal Warwickshire Regiment, 2/8th Worcestershire Regiment
183rd Brigade: 1/9th Royal Scots, 1/5th Gordon Highlanders, 1/8th Argyll & Sutherland Highlanders
184th Brigade: 2/5th Gloucestershire Regiment, 2/4th Royal Berkshire Regiment, 2/4th Oxford & Bucks Light Infantry

INDEX